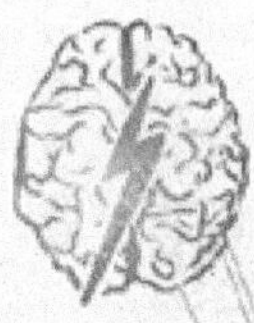

2ND EDITION

CREATE ROBUST REVENUE

Using Trust, Communication & Outsourced Gig Workforce

GRETCHEN GLASSCOCK

2ND EDITION

CREATE ROBUST REVENUE

Using Trust, Communication & Outsourced Gig Workforce

GRETCHEN GLASSCOCK

Printed in the United States.

Cover and book design by Asya Blue Design.

ISBN	978-1-7360176-4-7	Paperback
ISBN	978-1-7360176-3-0	Ebook

CONTENTS

PREFACE 1

I am, at heart, at this point in my career, a mentor. Or, at least, that is what I strive to be. I want to pass on to others, particularly to women and many minorities, the hard won skills and insights I have been able to acquire because, in part, I was fortunate enough to have been given many advantages and lucky enough to have been mentored by very generous and extremely knowledgeable business and professional colleagues.

Starting with my father, an outstandingly successful entrepreneur, who rose from being a farm boy through hard work, brains, and luck, to B.K Kleburg of the King Ranch family, scion of Texas legend, who took me under his wing and that of his entire "brain trust" type organization, to the last chapter of my instruction: the Webgrrls of California, early adopter tech types who saw a woman with zero tech skills and decided they would support my early efforts, before there were pre-made websites, or "what you see is what you get", or modules, now called widgets where you could just drag a piece of code where you wanted it on your web page and see whole wonderful art and sales pieces appear on your website.

I, on the other hand, in the early '90s, had to teach myself rudimentary HTML to make anything appear on a website, and, even then, some of the simplest code would not conform to what I wanted it to do because code does not do what you want it to do; it does what you tell it to do. And the Webgrrls were there for me. Somewhere, inside themselves, at some time in their life, they had probably struggled with something....not necessarily tech code.... and finally achieved a solution. And they were kind enough and compassionate enough to want to share the fruits and advantages they had acquired through the hard work of developing these skills. I was the lucky recipient. And now I want to do the same thing and "pay it forward", share these skills, techniques and insights with some who may not have had the advantages I've had. This book was written for them and for you, if you are one of them.

Sometimes I created my own mentors: business or tech experts I began to follow online in the new, digital frontier that had just opened up in the early 90's, or those business giants, from decades earlier, who had written books or had books written about them, who were neither geniuses or unicorns, which most of us, after all, are not, but who had achieved extraordinary success. Each of them had come up with some unique viewpoint or management technique , or perhaps a galaxy of them, that contributed to their success.

One mentor I adopted, at least in his strong preference for "bootstrapping" rather than taking money from investors, was "Mark Cuban an American billionaire entrepreneur, television personality, and media proprietor whose net worth is an estimated " $4 or 5 $4.3 billion. He laid out in Inc. magazine why he is against taking investors' money: *"Sweat Equity is always the best equity. The next best version of equity is Customer Equity where you get customers coming in buying from you and that's how you're funding your growth. Third is using kickstarter/IndieGogo as a way to support you. The last thing on the list is venture capital money"* and he goes on to explain why: in short, it robs your independence and puts you at someone else's mercy, not necessarily fulfilling your own vision which is probably why you wanted to start a business in the first place.

One of my most valuable mentors in learning to operate by outsourcing, was Harold Geneen, the legendary head of ITT (International Telegraph and Telephone Company) who, in the 70's, obviously decades earlier than the digital revolution, developed a management style that, at least for him, became a burgeoning factory turning out success after success. . He "transformed ITT from a troubled telecommunications firm with annual sales of $765 million to a global conglomerate with $22 billion in sales 17 years later". And there was no magic or rocket science to it, simply hard work, doing one's homework, "seat of the pants to seat of the chair", to develop very good communication that unearthed and highlighted all the relevant facts so one could make good decisions that solved a problem and created long term solutions.

I would say that one of the keys to Geneen's success was developing a short, simple "Management Report" that each of the hundreds of managers reporting to him turned in and he read, in order to keep up with the business and to help them make good decisions together. Geneen focused on tracking key performance indicators (KPIs) and having them presented in a clear, simple manner. Starting with a short summary of the KPIs at the top of the report, Geneen's goal was to increase efficiency and, whenever possible, improve his numbers. But, unlike many managers, Geneen did not get too technical. He believed *"The key, essential element in all good business management is emotional attitude. The rest is mechanics."*

Geneen believed delving into the real, underlying facts, led to good decisions. I remember reading of one occasion when no one in the companies involved could figure out why a certain forest operation in Canada kept losing money, despite all indications it should be making money. In the end, when management finally unearthed an answer, it was no giant technical insight. It stemmed from the fact, as they finally discovered, that the harshness of the weather in that location was inhibiting the growth of the trees, which became so stunted, they did not grow robustly and, consequently, did not produce enough wood to make the necessary profit. Geneen had just had to keep digging and drilling down through the facts. As he put it: "His decisions, (when) based realistically upon reliable information, were not all that difficult. Facts are power."

The secret sauce here was "Communication". It was by this method that Geneen always knew what was going on. And you can do the same, much easier today than in Geneen's pre-digital era. Just with a constant flow of emails, shared Google Docs, or an app that allows constant communication, sharing details on a continuous basis with your tech or outsourced talent allows both of you to make decisions in real time.

There was a time, when running a bit more formal business out of a corporate office, in management meetings, I basically used Geneen's rather short management reports, which led off with "Key Performance Indicators", principally the numbers and stats - a summary of the detailed information below, to elicit information from my associates or staff . As I moved into the digital era and digital work, as ecommerce and communication moved online, the relaying of information was much faster, almost instantaneous, and, in most cases for my small companies and tiny staff, at least daily or every few days. So, in multiple ways, communication became much easier. And, as people learn to relax and communicate with fewer filters, trust usually develops. Also, as more communication developed, with each staff member or outsourced talent, I began to know that person better, be more in tune with that person and recognize certain patterns, even though I might never have met that person, face to face, only in the digital world, working from distant , far flung countries and time zones. Sometimes I thought: "I've seen this movie before." Whenever I got an email that basically conveyed that a tech worker was trying to delegate something back to me...... and particularly remembering that the entire purpose of my delegating was so I could do more on a different level, so I had many different talented people I was delegating to... I had to react and get into corrective action. I eventually learned that whatever failure there was, was my fault. I had failed to explain something properly or see that the worker actually understood it. Sometimes I failed to recognize that even though a tech worker might be able to code 100 times or 1,000 times better than I could, it did not necessarily mean that he or she had experience knowing how to bring more traffic to a website or some other fairly specific commercial website, audience targeting technique. Once I owned this as my own fault, I would swing into my mentoring mode and be sure that the worker knew we were working on this together and we would solve it together. Just as he or she supported me, in achieving my website goals and boosting my knowledge to do so, I could be counted on to support him in understanding our goals, helping set them and helping work on them together. Once this was clear.... and that person could relax because it was no longer a short coming he was trying to hide or escape from... once we were truly working together in a collaborative way, we always succeeded, one way or another.

And the more success we have had , as an organization, the more trust develops between associates because whatever we are doing is working. And, in a fast paced, usually easily correctable environment, even failures can develop trust, because it is easier to spot them, work together, correct them and move on.

Attitude

As Geneen noted, *"The key, essential element in all good business management is emotional attitude. The rest is mechanics."*

I couldn't agree more. Many people, when they get involved in a technical business, or, in fact, any business, get caught up in all the technicalities and, that, at times, has included me. Sometimes it's easy or , at least, easier, to believe there is a "magic bullet" out there, that will make everything ok, that will make your business go swimmingly. There is not. Generally, there are a number of solutions that are workable and you just have to find the right one for you. In this book I am giving you examples of what means and methods, techniques and companies worked for me. They may not all work for you and certainly many of them won't , long term, or other companies will come along and improve on them, and you may try them , decide to use them, then you will be on a new track, your own track. But the methods that have worked for me will get you started and "there is magic in new beginnings."

"Have the Grit to Persist and You Will Succeed

Business is about problems. You will have problems to solve, day in, day out, every day you are in business. As the great manager of ITT, Harold Geneen, used to say "If you've tried 23 times and failed, you must try the 24th time. You must keep searching for a solution that is not just for the moment, but which is strategic and generic and forms a permanent solution to the problem."

You should also realize that success itself is about persistence. Not genius, or inspiration, or even abundant financing can take the place of persistence. The workplace is littered with failed geniuses or yesterday's stars who are today's old news. Persistence is the fuel that keeps the engine chugging up the hill. In the long run, it also helps to have integrity, to stick to your word with your employees and clients, who will then stick by you and your company, in both the peaks and the valleys. But to keep chugging ahead, and get past those many speed bumps, you will definitely need a large dose of persistence. Remember, you're in this for you, not for what others might think at any given moment; and you're in it for the long haul.

Whether it's a one-person shop juggling a dozen outsourced tasks, or a multi-million dollar enterprise setting new profit records, thousands of men and women today have made the decision to call their own shots, take the heat, and make the payroll, even if it's one outsourced person you've hired on Upwork or TaskRabbit. You are not alone. I hope the insights and techniques in this book will help you.

The Rest of the Journey - Achieving Balance: The 20% Solution

It's not easy to have a successful business, do what you love, be busy all the time, and still get what you really want out of life. In my case, I have been fortunate because I was able to get in on the ground floor of the Internet, before big commercial companies came in to compete. My first website had four million visitors the first month and crashed the server three times. A global audience of women was hungry for the kind of information AdvancingWomen.com offered. We explained to women how to use the new tools on the Net to reach out, network, get a mentor, balance work and family, and keep moving up the ladder. My site went on to be written up in national and international media, and I was doing business in about 12 of the 24 time zones on Earth. I had successfully created a robust revenue stream. You can do the same. It's even much, much easier now that a digital revolution has taken place and many, very simple user tools are available to get you on the Net, as well as a thriving "gig" or freelance worker economy is available globally, providing the support you need, at competitive prices you select to pay.

Once you succeed, however, one challenge will be to make this new challenge work for your life, and help you achieve balance. Even with outsourced teams of talented specialists, including designers, technologists, and programmers, I pulled many all-nighters, and found myself constantly overbooked and over busy. I didn't mind the fast pace as much as I did finally realizing that as much as I loved my business—which was also a passion to help level the playing field for women in careers and business—I was missing many of life's pleasures. I wasn't spending enough quality time with my family and friends.

I traveled to places such as the White House for conferences about helping women in emerging nations build their businesses; to Madeleine Albright's luncheons on advancing in politics; to American Educational Research conferences to speak and support global research on women's issues, and to Brussels, Belgium, and other venues to teach businesswomen how to use technology on the Net. But I no longer had time or energy to travel to Europe and some of the cultural meccas I loved to explore, or simply to lie on the beach or on a ship deck headed to anywhere to just relax and recharge.

I had been brought up in a money savvy family, so I knew the many benefits of developing a passive income, and I'd done it before. But my fascination and absorption with the Net at each of its evolving stages and the powerful new tools and apps that appeared in an unceasing flow had led me to lose my way and step on a treadmill of constant work. It was time to step off!

Since that realization, I have put into practice the 20 percent solution. I have made it a practice to develop passive income streams from the Net, using no more than 20 percent of my time to manage the revenue streams I diligently created. I've learned to make my website work smarter, not harder, and accomplish my income goals in an effective, systematic way. I've learned to put efficient systems and automated pieces of code on a website to do the enormous amount of smart work it once took an army of highly paid programmers to do.

As an entrepreneur, I have always been on the lookout for ways to do things better, faster, and less expensively, and I want to share this with others so they will not have to go through the pain of trying to figure it out. The work to create a website has to be done once, but then the income continues to flow. With this approach I can continue doing the work I love, but less of it, giving me more time to do other things I enjoy in life. I want you to be able to do the same.

There are simple, logical steps to setting up this passive revenue stream.

- Identify a niche market.
- Discover and hone your own brand.
- Automate as many processes as possible.
- Outsource.
- Market.
- Use the Pareto Principle, 80/20 to focus on only your most profitable business.
- Use the Pareto Principle, 80/20 to spend 20 percent of your time working.

The goal should not be how much money you can make, but to make enough money to sustain the lifestyle you want. This might not include a Porsche, a villa in Italy, or trips to Paris or Milan to catch the designer collections. But it definitely can include stability, adventure, travel, fine wine, and the occasional splurge, with as little effort and as few wasted motions as possible.

Who I Am and Why You Should Believe Me

I was a web professional, earning a living on the Net for over 20 years. My websites won Lycos Top 5 percent award, Dow Jones award, Beatrice Yahoo top site, and WWWomen Best of Net, with one listed in Femina as a top women's career site. I have been featured in *Elle, Self, Women, SUCCESS,* and *Fast Company* magazines, among many others.

I have been involved as a website and web community creator in the formative phase of the Net, and I have experienced and participated in each phase of its growth and evolution. This deep experience has enabled me to work on the Net in a way that fuses strategic business processes with powerful new Net platforms and cutting-edge technology.

I can either show you how to build your first website or show you how to adapt your present site to make it work better to accomplish your goals.

Who Should Read This

- If you have a passion and want to start a blog to share your thoughts with others
- If you are mapping out your career path and want to broadcast your value • If you already have a blog and want to monetize it
- If you have a passion to be an entrepreneur and start your own business
- If you are a stay-at-home mom or dad and want to start earning money from home
- If your company downsized and you want to earn on your own
- If you have an existing business and want to take it online
- If you have an online business and want to kick it up a notch
- If you are a busy, but harried professional, looking for more work-life balance

I know how challenging it is to launch or redirect your career or to start a new business and how many questions need to be answered to get you to where you want to go. This book will show you how to start, put the pieces together, launch, and successfully manage a low-maintenance, revenue-producing, online business. I've done it many times, for myself and others. I will do it for you. Let me show you the "big picture" and the specific step-by-step details.

Goal—To Create Multiple Revenue Streams That Can Become Passive Income

Overall Strategy

To discover a profitable niche that suits you and your interests. In order to sustain a website with continuous updates in content that provide value to your audience, it is essential that you have a deep and abiding interest in your subject. You will also be tracking results and tweaking many aspects of the site to enhance viewer engagement and continuously improve traffic.

If you select a subject just to make money, you'll likely run out of steam along the way. Building a profitable website, your authority about the subject, and development of loyal followers are long-term projects, so be sure you are committed to the subject matter.

Design

Don't be intimidated by the many great-looking websites you may see on the Net. You don't need to possess great design skills yourself. There are many attractive, practical, and effective professionally designed themes available on the Net (many of them free), which can give your site the attractiveness and polish you need. This book offers some details about what to look for in designs and where to find them.

Automation

As much automation as possible is essential for developing passive income. Automation for producing content, products, service, and selling will help leverage your time and efforts. Using your website to automate routine tasks enables you to accomplish the greatest amount of work with the least wasted motion. The fewer people you need to hire, the more effective and profitable your business will be.

Outsourcing

At first, if you're not comfortable with some technical tasks, you may prefer to outsource them. Later, after you've developed your business to a point where you need help to handle it, you should turn to outsourcing in order to have a flexible staff and a flexible payroll, so you only have to spend money when you have revenue that more than covers your expenses. If you need to get some work done immediately, so you will have time to read this book, go directly to Chapter 7 on Outsourcing.

CHAPTER 1

WHY START YOUR OWN BUSINESS?

WANT TO DEVELOP A ROBUST & RELIABLE LIVING & DO IT YOUR WAY?

STOP TRADING HOURS FOR DOLLARS

I think we can agree—jobs are dependent on someone giving you one, and also keeping you in it. What I want you to realize is that you can create a job for yourself that no one can take away. You can start your own business and employ yourself. You have it within your power to take charge of your work life.

Now might be the perfect moment to start your own business. It can be after hours or after your day job, to start out. Think of it as an opportunity to fulfill your dreams while maintaining your cash flow and your responsibilities in your day job. Or think of it as a life raft, in case your boat (your main job) sinks, which, unfortunately, is something that could happen to any of us, at any time.

When the economy heads south, as it does from time to time, everyone's job (outside of civil service, health care, possibly teaching, and a few other fields) is about as stable as a Slinky, headed down five flights of stairs...you never know where it might land, or when it will either cascade or fall to the bottom.

So, starting up a second revenue-producing machine, in the form of your own business, could be a really good investment of your time and resources. You will achieve more independence and flexibility, better balance for work and family, become CEO of your own firm, and, (where there is risk, there is reward) you could become quite rich. But, at the least, you will be doing something you enjoy, have your independence, and be in charge of your life. If you want a vacation, just take it! If you have a project or a client you don't enjoy working on or with, drop them. Scale up or scale down as you wish. That is the path to a more satisfying life, both at work and at home.

Getting Rich

Paul Sloane, at LifeHack.org, starts off "The Six Best Ways to Get Rich" by saying, "We tend to assume that if we work hard and save money then one day we will end up wealthy.

This is wishful thinking. We are more likely to end up with some modest but useful savings. If you want to accumulate serious wealth then there [are] a number of approaches you can use and some are much more effective than others."

In my view, the most likely approaches for the majority of people are the two following paths, which Sloane defines:

1. **"Start your own business and eventually sell it.** This is the most effective and proven way to become rich. If you can find a new approach to customer's needs and build a profitable business that addresses that need then you have created real value. It could be a cleaning business, a hairdresser's, a consultancy or an investment bank. It will probably take years of very hard work to build up the enterprise. Most new businesses fail so the risks are high. You need all the skills, dynamism, perseverance and diligence of an entrepreneur. But if you can pull it off the potential rewards are huge. This is how many of the seriously wealthy people did it."

Of course, most people don't have the risk tolerance to start their own business and many lack the tenacity to stick with it, so this will be the minority. But many believe it to be a happy minority because, even if they don't get rich by selling it, they are doing what they want and at the very least, have their independence and a business capable of sustaining them.

To launch that business, you must identify a product or service that is related to your unique niche and becomes the central topic of your website.

2. **"Exploit your skill as a self-employed expert.** If you can develop a marketable skill and retain your independence then you can reap considerable rewards. This is how sports stars, authors and entertainers become rich. In general the self-employed expert has greater earnings opportunities

than one who works for a company. There are risks and you have to have something special. Your success is in your own hands so this is a popular route for people who have developed a skill and want to strike out on their own."

This second path is to "super size" your career, so the product is you. You do this by packaging yourself as an expert in your field and selling your services. Of course, you must have the skills and credentials to back it up, and you will need to create a website platform and social media marketing to reach out and broadcast your skills to a defined target market.

I've done this too—leveraging my experience and expertise in creating and running a web business to answer the call when clients asked me to build simple, flexible, easy-to-manage website platforms for whatever the client wanted to promote and sell. I built them for other individuals, universities, national associations and businesses, both national and international. If people are looking for a solution, and you have one and get the word out, people will turn to you to solve their problem. It's a simple formula, with one key ingredient: credibility. You have to be able to deliver.

Based on decades of business experience and in-depth research by some of the leading organizations in the nation devoted to this issue, there are proven strategies along a continuum that become a successful career path (Advancing Women dubbed this the "pipeline to empowerment," including research, skills development, leadership training, visibility, and alliances. But there generally comes a time in your career where you reach a "fork in the road" or a "decision point," where you must decide if you are going to continue on your career track or if you are going to establish a business to codify, package, broadcast, and make a profit from what you know, your skills, and your expertise in your own field.

To start your own business you have to leave the comfort zone of college, your home, a big corporation, or even a nonprofit or any other type of salaried employment. In exchange, you have independence and the chance to pursue your dream. The flip side is that you no longer have large resources—money, manpower, credit, expertise, contacts, or name recognition—all you have is … you.

The thought that keeps most entrepreneurs motivated at those first insecure moments is the firm knowledge that great risk can reap great rewards. Studies have shown that entrepreneurs come in all shapes and sizes, all temperaments and work methods. Some are deliberate and painstakingly meticulous in drawing up a five-year business plan. Others fly by the seat of their pants and say "Let's just do it." Some are exuberant, some quiet. Some extroverts, some introverts. Some are workaholics; some just spend enough time to delegate the work to the right people whom they've had the ability and insight to select. There is only one thing all entrepreneurs have in common—the ability and willingness to take risks.

Part of the decision-making process must be you looking deep inside yourself and facing honestly just how much risk you can tolerate. People who are most comfortable being entrepreneurs are those who have a high tolerance for the unstructured and learn to accept ambiguity. They decide to take each day as it comes, work on their strategic planning, be obsessive about details, produce the best quality product or service they can, market aggressively, track the numbers, and believe the business will come.

Whether you want to strike out on your own as an entrepreneur or enhance your career as an expert, reaping rewards on the side, you will need a platform to broadcast your expertise. This book will help you build an effective platform to reach those goals.

How to Start

Start from where you are with what you have. Use the information in this book to create a simple website. Put your product or service out there on the web and see if people like it. If they do, then keep leveraging up.. You can and should leverage up for the life of the site to keep it fresh, interesting, constantly evolving, and compelling.

Want to Get Rich? Stop Trading Hours for Dollars

If you work and are paid by the hour, your income is limited by the number of working hours you have at your disposal. Like everyone else, all you have is time and your time is finite. If, however, you are able somehow to expand the time available to you, without expending any more effort or acquiring any more skills or expertise—becoming a brain surgeon, for instance, or an estate attorney for the seriously affluent, or a used car magnate—you will be able to earn more.

How do you do this? How do you expand your time? Every affluent person knows the answer to this. One way or another, you have to find a way to climb out of the traditional and perpetual trading-hours-for-dollars method of earning money. This is like shoveling coal into an old-fashioned locomotive; you shovel, the coal burns, then you shovel some more. Yes, you can earn *some* money that way but only with your core expertise. Don't stop doing it—at least, not yet. Keep your day job, if you have one, and let that money be your launching pad.

Here's how the people who start climbing toward wealth do it. Take Anna. Let's say she's a seamstress. She makes so many dollars per hour sewing. She buys a sewing machine and the automation allows her to work faster and make more money. She is able to hire more workers, buy more machines, and the next thing you know she has a small factory. Anna is now able to use her time training others, moving from doing to delegating, overseeing quality, and spreading the word about her sewing enterprise. Business picks up. Anna is starting to make a lot more money.

Anna is on her way to attaining wealth because she was able to stop trading hours for dollars. How did she do this? She had a skill and developed a reputation around the quality of her skill. She could have raised her prices incrementally and continued to get more customers but, in the end, she would have been limited by the time she had available to work.

Instead, she invested in automation and labor, which freed up her time to market her services. All her customers knew Anna, liked the quality of her work, and felt comfortable that if they dealt with her, she would guarantee good quality. They didn't care who sewed the material or what brand of sewing machine they used.

Whether you are an online entrepreneur or a work-at-home parent, you can do the same thing. Once you have established your business and built it up to a certain point, you have some choices to expand your supply of time so you can do what you do best, which is probably to design, produce, sell, and maintain the quality of your product or service. Here's how:

1. Automate.

- Automate as many tasks as possible.
- Consider putting all your bills on autopay..
- If you're not a techie, ask a local tech guru or college student to set up as many automated features as possible on your computer.
- Have emails with a certain subject line go into a dedicated email folder.
- Set up an autoresponder with a series of messages that fit your most common situations. (Most of the email marketing systems, such as Constant Contact or AWeber offer auto responders. You are going to need an email marketing system anyway to automate your marketing and sales, so you should take full advantage of it to automate your customer communications.)
- Set up a phone service with an 800 number with a cloud service. I use RingCentral so I'm not distracted by phone calls and then I have large, uninterrupted blocks of time to work. The best time management advice is "Don't answer your phone except during a certain, designated time each day when you return calls." Also, my goal is to have a paperless office. For many years, these RingCentral apps sat on my desktop, ready for fast, easy chores, although Faxes generally have been replaced by email attachments,

but are still used by some government and medical offices.

- If you have a Smartphone or an iPhone, use it as a virtual assistant for as many tasks as possible, such as reminders or scheduling appointments.

RingCentral

2. Outsource.

Give up all the routine, administrative work someone else can do for you: from setting up online accounts, to inserting RSS feeds into Twitter Feed, or specialized tech work, there's someone out there you can find through Upwork TaskRabbit,

Amazon Mechanical Turk, or Fiverr who can do it better and faster to free up your time to create, oversee, and market, which pays a lot more.

3. Use Tools Designed to Pare Down Your Work.

You definitely will need to be on top of your accounting, so you might want to go with the industry standard, Intuit's QuickBooks online, used by more than half of all small businesses. The program stores your data in a cloud service starting at $12.50 a month, with a free trial. It tracks sales, accepts payments, and can handle payroll for you.

Ideally you won't have a payroll, but instead will deploy contract labor for specific tasks. Work executed by providers on freelance sites, such as Upwork or TaskRabbit will be paid through those services' payment systems, or one they use, such as PayPal. Although many of my payments are handled through these systems, I also use FreshBooks for projects, such as consulting or website creation, because I like its ease of use and time tracking automation.

Logged hours are automatically put into your timesheet for that client. With either system you put the information in once, then let a system track time, log expenses, and invoice your clients with a few clicks. Both platforms offer a free 30-day trial, and after that, with FreshBooks, the first three clients are free, giving you an opportunity to build your cash flow before you start paying for a service. These types of accounting and invoicing services lend a professional polish to your business and are critical to your success, because they help you track your expenses and make sure you are actually making a profit on what you sell.

4. Offload non-essential tasks.

This means getting rid of anything that's a time consumer and not an income producer, including tasks in your personal life. I hope you're not still mowing your own lawn or cleaning your own house if you're trying to start, grow, or run a business at the same time. I have a friend who works at a top national radio chain. She pointed out that the common denominator of every successful female executive she knew was that they had household help. You should aspire to do the same, if not in the beginning, at least as soon as you are able.

5. Invest for Passive Income.

Aside from the fact that you want to save and invest, you want your money to be working for you. It's the same principle as hiring an employee or contract labor: someone else is carrying some of the load, while you are out doing what you do best. And your hours have been stretched. Plus, if you're ever injured or can't or don't want to work, investments producing passive income keep working for you.

6. Diversify.

My father used to say that you should always have at least three businesses, because there was never a time when one of them wasn't doing badly. Translated into today's professional language, instead of three businesses, one might say three revenue streams. It's the same principle as not having only one big client. What do you do when they drop you, hire their brother-in-law, or go under? What do you do when one revenue stream dries up or sinks like a rock in a river? Better have another to fall back on.

This is simple to do on the web because a good website will support multiple income streams. Example: your main product or service is one income stream; ad revenue from Google AdSense and private advertisers is another; affiliate revenue, at the very least from Amazon, which, from its thousands of products, surely has one or more that matches your target demographic.

Lessons from My Business

In my web business, **I devote my skills and attention to the creation or curation of high quality content, graphics, and business processes for my website(s) or a website or blog I am producing, consulting on, or overseeing for another organization. Someone else can do the rest.** I do some of the tech aspects because I had to learn to do them when the web was still getting cranked up and there were few techs and no automated software around. But if I can pay someone, say $300 to handle a tech piece, while I am creating, say $1,000 or $1,200 in revenue, or even $3,500 to $8,000 on building a client's website, that seems to me like a pretty good trade for everybody. The tech gets more jobs, the client gets a great product faster, and I create more revenue for my company. **Everybody wins. Right?**

Work Out a Lean, Mean Business Model with a One Page Plan

The goal of this business model is to skip the old fashioned 25+ page business plan. Identify all your activities, costs, revenue streams, and value proposition in this one-page Business Model Canvas Template.

Train yourself to be aware of all the factors that can impact your business. Keep your options open and be ready to respond with lightning speed, because the need to survive comes before anything else. Cash flow trumps profitability, at least in the beginning. Focus like a laser. Fill out this one-page business plan to get started. *But carry a big eraser.*

Show it to friends and associates. Get some honest feedback and keep honing it. There are a lot of moving parts to a business plan, and you will have to keep adjusting your model to the realities on the ground and what the market is telling you.

Over time, a market can change or you might move to a new locale. Or different products might trigger different preferences. How your customer wants to communicate with you might change. For example, the spiraling number of Smartphones led to the explosive growth of the mobile web, the dawn of mobile payment processing, and has changed how customers want to do business with you.

Be sure to review your business plan regularly to be sure you are taking all these marketing changes into account and also engaging in a process of continuous improvement.

Creative Commons License

You can download this template and work out your own plan.

How Much Money Will You Need to Start?

Because that is relative, let's first look at some comparisons.

If you want to build a passive income from owning stocks or bonds, you will have to accumulate a lot of capital to start. To achieve $50,000 a year of annual income at 1 percent, you would need to invest $5 million dollars, a sum most of us don't have lying around waiting to put to good use. To generate $50,000 a year at 5 percent, you would need to have $1 million invested, also a bit of a stretch for most of us.

Let's say you want to buy into a franchise: generally it will cost you a lot. Here are Denny's requirements, at the time of this writing:

"**Denny's is seeking franchise partners who understand the restaurant business**.

Minimum Financial Requirements
(Can include partners and companies)
$350,000 liquid capital to invest
$1,000,000 net worth

Preferred Experience
Restaurant / retail management
Total Estimated Initial Investment
$1,200,000 to $2,600,00

Franchise Fee
$35,000 "

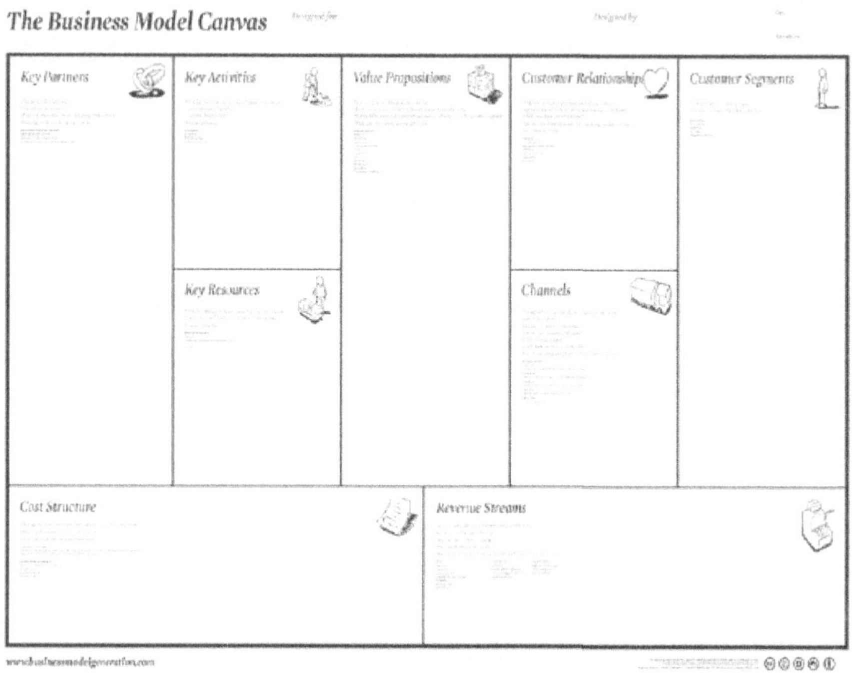

Although these are the terms Denny's is offering the public, I'm not suggesting this is the only deal that can be had at Denny's. Many of these franchisors offer special deals and financing to valued and hardworking employees. If you work at a franchise, you might investigate.

One guarantee you will get buying into a franchise is that you will have to work extremely hard. And, if you don't understand the restaurant business—one of the most challenging around—you are pretty much out of luck. I do know someone who became seriously affluent leveraging up her Denny's franchises—she now owns Denny's in , I believe, 8 states—but she is not only smart and a hard worker, she started out as a waitress and can look at a restaurant and know exactly what it will take to succeed.

You can also buy a house and rent it out. In my market, in San Antonio, Texas, in 2021, for a minimum of about $250,000, plus the cost of furnishings, if you're ambitious, resourceful, have good taste or turn to someone who does; can identify a fixer-upper in an up-and-coming or rapidly regentrifying neighborhood; have the patience to endure the ordeal of working with contractors and go through a smart but thrifty renovation process; you can probably bring in a post-rent revenue of possibly $2000 to $2800 a month plus the benefit of a few write-offs.

On the other hand, for comparison, you can build an attractive website that cap tures eyeballs, brings in revenue, and turns a profit for $500 to a few thousand dollars start-up costs , depending on what software and templates you purchase, how much help you need, plus plenty of "sweat equity." I know. I've done it—many times. This is because you are using "intellectual capital," all the things you have learned throughout your life, then leveraging them in a practical way with the product or service your website offers.

Ultimately, your return on investment (ROI) is likely to be much greater than other investments, although it is unlikely you would be able to scale them beyond a certain size. In other words, you might be able to make a reasonable or even healthy income for yourself, but you will not be able to become a Google, Yahoo, or Facebook without a lot more investment.

But a website needn't be your only investment. You can have a website and a rental house or a stock market account, if you choose. And, of course, I recommend you do, if you can swing it, even if you start small. Perhaps you have a garage apartment or a basement you can rent. Most people can accumulate $500 or $1,000 and invest in an index fund or mutual fund that suits you, then leverage up.

As for start-up money, I agree with Mark Cuban who said: "**Rule #1: Sweat Equity is the best start up capital....** There are only two reasonable sources of capital for startup entrepreneurs, your own pocket and your customers' pock ets.... You shouldn't have to take money from anyone. Businesses don't have to start big. The best ones start small enough to suit the circumstances of their founders.... As much as you want to think that all things would change if you only had more cash available, they probably won't. **The reality is that for most businesses, they don't need more cash, they need more brains"**.

To go the Mark Cuban boot-strapping route, you will need to make some basic decisions about how to run your company. If you run it with an eye toward thrift, which resembles a tiger protecting her young, pay cash as often as you can, do more things yourself, outsource, don't pay for fancy trappings, flashy stationary, or lunches out with people you want to impress—impress them with your profits instead—you will have a better, more stress-free chance of making it to the finish line a winner.

In fact, if there was only one mistake I could steer you away from it would be this: thinking that in order to succeed, you need to spend more. It is always tempting to think there are "silver bullets" that will create instant success, but that is totally discredited by reality. If there is any kind of slow-motion "silver bullet," it is the opposite.

It's hanging onto your money so you can keep slowly and painstakingly building your business, based on the value you provide. (And I speak as one who survived the dot-com crash and a whole host of others in various industries, each thought to be a catastrophic devastation and they were, for those who had no cash left to maintain, regroup, and rebuild as the dust settled.)

So Don't Raise Money—Bootstrap a Niche Market

CHAPTER 2

DEFINE YOUR NICHE

FIGURE OUT YOUR CORE COMPETENCE CONSIDER WHAT PROCESSES YOU ARE REALLY GOOD AT

So Don't Raise Money—Bootstrap A Niche Market

Many entrepreneurs are willing to risk their careers, their homes, and their families, and work until they drop, in order to own their own businesses. The problem is there are a lot of really big players with million or even billion-dollar deep pockets chasing the same markets. What to do? One answer is to think small, or at least smaller. Consider a "niche" market.

Define Your Niche

First you have to discover what your niche should be. One way to approach this is to zero in on what niche you would excel in, which would make the most of your own special knowledge and talents. You might be really creative, extremely organized, or able to rally people together to work on a specific project or cause. Being smart about specific, marketable things has value; it is "the raw material from which financial results are produced." Taking a hard, objective look at yourself, assembling a knowledge-and-skills inventory, allows you to find your particular niche, something you do better than others in your same field. It is a way of narrowing and refining your niche so you can focus on only those things you do best and know more about than those around you. This should tell you what niche market you should target.

Sometimes this happens in a more evolutionary way. You set up a dot com on the Net to sell a certain genre of books and the next thing you know, Amazon. com turns into Godzilla, about to stamp you under its giant foot, selling the same genre of books and many of the same titles. Do you stand there, stare

Amazon. com in the eye and go head-to-head in combat? You do no such thing. You think through your special niche and move a step farther in that direction, away from the center and away from Amazon.

Let's say you start marketing rare old books. If Amazon.com moves in that direction, you start marketing rare old books on Texana, a quite profitable business. In other words, you keep moving another step away from the center of the market. And eventually you'll find a niche that is too small for Amazon.com but might be specialized enough so that it requires considerable expertise for entry.

That is a drama that played out between a cloud storage tech company, Rackspace, and several of the tech giants. Rackspace first developed a market for the "cloud," online storage, and, in no time at all, the big boys (Amazon, Google, and Microsoft) wanted a piece of that market. Rackspace, finding itself seriously outgunned financially, tried to focus on its" fanatical customer service," to carve out a competitive niche for itself, one where it felt it could outperform the big boys. That, however, was not a very viable long term strategy.

Rackspace's stock price plummeted. Its a market capitalization is dwarfed by some of the bigger players ; it is, for example . a fraction of that of Amazon.

Rackspace is still searching for a way to differentiate itself and its survival depends on that. That's the route any company will have to take: discovering and leveraging your "Unique Selling Point" (USP), a quality or skill that allows you to outperform others in the market. You will have to dig deep into yourself to find the area you can execute better than most people, a market too small for the giants, but extremely profitable, perhaps because you have the field almost to yourself. Build a solid reputation for excellence and the giants might even send people your way for products they don't stock or services they choose not to offer.

Brand Yourself as Well as Your Product

Create your own personal brand in order to stand out from the crowd and capture the attention of your audience. Few have done this better than Christiane Amanpour.

When we think of Amanpour, what comes to mind? An attractive, sophisticated woman in a safari shirt and jeans in some exotic locale—perhaps the Middle East—engaging in incisive commentary on world events, comfortable asking probing questions of world leaders, often in moments of crisis. Amanpour is one of the most recognized international journalists on American television, with a willingness to work in dangerous conflict zones.

She's created a name for herself in exploring and analyzing the issues behind international hotspots, such as the Middle East. Or you might see her donning a burka to covertly explore the tormented and male-dominated society in Afghanistan. And these days, she often jumps into CNN's round tables to help analyze domestic political issues or current events. She speaks English, Persian, and French fluently.

That is who we think of when we think of Amanpour. Her name doesn't bring to mind images of her as a wife and mother, which she also is, or arriving at an international soiree in elegant evening attire and striking jewelry, which she also does. Chatting and dishing with the ladies on *The View?* No. She may have pivoted a bit to interviews on international issues where she made a name for herself. But, with all the pivots available to her, Amanpour has succeeded in creating her personal brand and melding it seamlessly with her professional life. You can do the same.

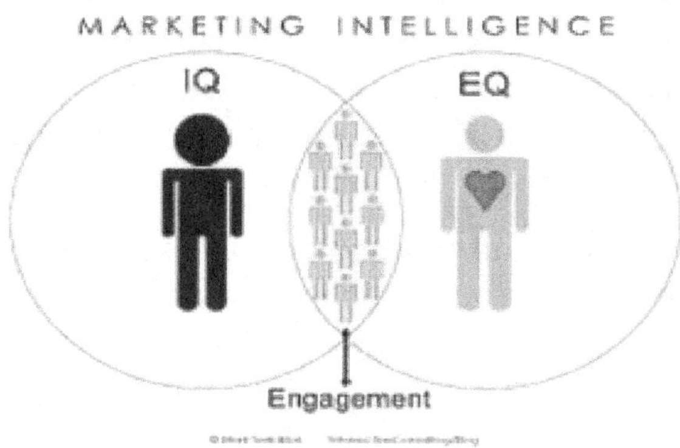

Marketing Intelligence (Photo credit: Intersection Consulting)

First Identify, then Reinforce and Broadcast Your Brand

Seth Godin, marketer extraordinaire and Internet guru, makes the case that, when trying to figure out the direction you need to go in your work life, you need to look at two things: content/domain knowledge and process. He explains that process "refers to the emotional intelligence skills you have about managing projects, visualizing success, persuading other people of your point of view, dealing with multiple priorities etc."

Seth Godin, in his blog "What are you good at?" discusses the distinction: "Consider the difference between process and content.

Content is domain knowledge. People you know or skills you've developed. Playing the piano or writing copy about furniture sales. A rolodex of movers in a given industry, or your ability to compute stress ratios in your head.

Domain knowledge is important, but it's (often) easily learnable.

Process, on the other hand, refers to the emotional intelligence skills you have about managing projects, visualizing success, persuading other people of your point of view, dealing with multiple priorities, etc. This stuff is insanely valuable and hard to learn....

As the world changes ever faster, as industries shrink and others grow, process ability is priceless. Figure out which sort of process you're world-class at and get even better at it. Then, learn the domain... that's what the internet is for.

One of the reasons that super-talented people become entrepreneurs is that they can put their process expertise to work in a world that often undervalued it".

Because I grew up in a very business-oriented family I was raised to be an entrepreneur. That is, I was raised to start from where I was with what I had: work hard, assume nothing, reach out and talk to everyone who knew anything, be analytical, but most of all, have a bias toward action, think on your feet, and never assume there's a "silver bullet." When I was between five and ten years old, my father took me out, pointed at a building and asked, "What is that building worth?" The correct answer was "As much as someone will pay for it." That was a short lesson in supply and demand and also price elasticity.

From that starting point, I went on to work in several different industries, all of which I began with no domain knowledge whatsoever. What I had was what every entrepreneur needs: a tolerance for risk; a grounding in simple arithmetic, which will tell you most of the time whether you are on the right track or not; an ability to negotiate; and an absolute certainty I could learn or identify someone who already knew the essentials needed to succeed in whatever field I found myself. I knew I could because my father had convinced me I could. Not that I didn't have some failures, flame outs, and tough speed bumps along the way. We all do. But I learned from them and persevered and, invariably, went on to better things.

Art of the Incremental: Start with Your Core Competency

Entrepreneurs have been doing this for centuries: starting from where they are with what they've got and seeing what works. This is a time-tested process: if you want to start a business you do two things:

1. **Analyze** the true nature of your unique assets and core competencies to figure out how they can become a basis for a business.
2. **Try small,** low-stakes testing in the actual marketplace to determine what actually works. Then do more of what works and cut the losers. Keep doing low stakes testing and raise the ante on the winners.

My businessman father *insisted* I learn to play poker because it was like the game of business. It's not about the cards you're dealt but how you place your bets. Research shows, if 1,000 hands are dealt to four players, each will come out with about the same number of potentially winning hands. You have to be fearless, keeping your emotions under control and, hopefully, your poker face; you have to analyze how your competition plays and what your odds are of winning each hand, based both on the other players' behaviors and the statistical odds of poker, which you can brush up on by Googling the net or buying a paperback or Kindle book on Amazon. You fold on bad cards and quietly build the pot on the almost sure winning hands.

While I am making the business-poker analogy, I would also advise against putting all your chips in on any one hand, however bullet-proof it seems. The moment you bet your last chip on a full house, another player might well pull out four aces or a straight. Your goal is to stay in the game and win as many hands as possible. In business, as in poker, when you run out of cash, they take you out of the game.

As you practice the art of the incremental, you will be learning your business from the ground up, and you will soon learn when to hold 'em and when to fold 'em. But, my advice is to start small and build gradually.

How will you know what products or services to offer? Unless your customers have been asking for a particular product or service from you, you might not know. You will have to rely on small-scale testing. "Starve the problems; feed the opportunities."

Research not only helps, it is essential. It is not enough to just identify a product or service that suits you. You have to find something that suits you AND something that is also in demand that people are searching for on the Internet. Then you have to think through what kind of people are searching for this item so you can identify your target market and know who you are addressing in your blog posts.

For example, a housewife looking for recipes or cleaning tips or coupons to save money at the grocery store would be a different audience than an auto mechanic comparing tool sets. You should also analyze how much your target market is willing to pay, so you are offering a product in the right price range.

Establish Your Niche—Learn How to Differentiate Brand "You"

We all have a brand. Some of us just may not know it. And that's not a good thing. How are you going to shape and control your brand if you're not even aware of it? Or how can you put some energy and focus into getting it right?

You should become aware of your brand and focus on shaping it and broadcasting it. We all should. And, to achieve successful branding, we need to be able to differentiate our brand from all the other brands out there.

Why do you think you never see Christiane Amanpour interviewing a group of chefs on a cooking show or contestants on a game show? Because that's not her brand.

And whatever you may think of Miley Cyrus, she has done a bang-up job of transforming her image from sweet young Hannah Montana, to "What is she going to do next?" and "What's with that tongue?" Miley, the adult.

To examine branding a little more closely let's take a look at food conglomerate Kraft Foods, which sells hundreds of different food items in 155 countries—everything from A.1.Steak Sauce to Jell-O, Planters peanuts, and Velveeta.

Ok. A little further down that food chain, General Foods International is a subdivision of Kraft Foods and it produces several different flavors of instant coffee, everything from Cafe Vienna, Dark Mayan Chocolate, Hazelnut Belgian Cafe, Italian Cappuccino, Pumpkin Spice, to Vanilla Caramel Latte. Not much chance of mistaking Dark Mayan Chocolate with Pumpkin Spice, right?

And it should be the same with each of us. Our potential audiences, customers, or clientele should know, instantly, whether we are Dark Mayan Chocolate or Pumpkin Spice, metaphorically speaking.

For instance, I have operated a number of websites, one of which was AdvancingWomen.com. It dealt with career and financial parity for women by electronically mentoring them so they had the tools and training to get better jobs or start their own businesses. Occasionally I mentioned women running for political office, because, research shows, women legislators will pass laws more supportive of women. Fighting for equal pay would be one example.

No one on the web confused AdvancingWomen.com with a homemaking site. No one went there for gossip or make-up tips or adorable kitten photos, however popular any of those might be. People knew what AdvancingWomen.com was. The site might have had a small slice of a large pie, but it definitely had a slice. I didn't aim to gobble up the whole pie and lose even my slice in the food fight that could follow. As Esther Dyson, venture capitalist and digital guru said, "More companies die from indigestion than starvation." In other words, they take on too much and flame out or stumble trying to handle it all.

So the bottom line is to look deep inside yourself and decide who you are. Narrow your focus. Concentrate on that. That will be "Brand You." Broadcast that and you will succeed.

CHAPTER 3

START WITH THE BASICS

WHAT DO I SELL?

HOW TO RESEARCH DON'T MARRY IT, TEST IT

We understand that many people who *could* succeed as entrepreneurs *don't* succeed because they never get started. Almost 35 percent say they don't know where to start.

Well, that part is easy. It's particularly easy because many people have a limited number of options. No giant inheritance. No trust fund. No nest egg. No investors lined up and out through the door. So, start from where you are, with what you have. Keep it simple. There are lots of more complex, fleshed-out methods of telling you the same thing: plan a lean startup and begin with your "minimum viable product." Recognize that this will be a journey of trial and error, and you must listen to what the market—your customers—tell you and adjust your product or service accordingly.

It's Not Just a Website, It's a Business

This is a good place to start when one is considering how to approach constructing a website: understand it's not just a website, it's a business. Your website is a *reflection* of your business. If you don't have a viable business model—a way to produce income sufficient to sustain and grow your business—then you can put up an attractive website and hit all the marks, even bring in a ton of traffic, and it still won't achieve your goals.

Before you launch your website, think through, in advance, what your source of revenue will be. To produce a sustainable revenue stream from your website, you have to know what business you're in. You have to know who your clients or customers are and how to converse with them on the web. Then, if you are on your own, you have to embed your *business* processes and methods into your website. These will consist, in part, of certain plugins that have various functions, including broadcasting new posts to Google, building your email list, and broadcasting content to social media sites. Those are the hooks that will make you money.

Three Main Categories of Internet Start Ups

Broadly speaking, although there may be combinations and nuances, there are basically three broad categories of Internet startups. TechCrunch has described the following three categories, each with its unique characteristics and requirements for success:

> As a consumer Internet company, you are trying to attract enough potential customers by providing one (or more) of three kinds of products: 1) media, 2) premium services, or 3) access to a physical good. These are not mutually exclusive—a startup can generate revenue from more than one of these sources. For example, many media companies make

money off of both advertising and premium services, like LinkedIn.

1. Media:

If you are a media company, you are providing free content and collecting purchasing intent so that you can either sell ads, send leads to products or services your audience might be interested in, and/or upsell to a subscription or digital goods. This category comprises a large percentage of consumer Internet startups because startup costs are typically the lowest.

2. Paid Service:

If you provide a paid service, you are trying to attract as many potential consumers to you as cost effectively as possible, get them to pay you for a service, and then work to keep them as paying subscribers for as long as possible. Most startups in this arena follow the "Freemium" strategy, where some content or basic service is provided for free in the hopes of converting a small portion of the free base to paying subscribers.

3. Physical Commerce:

If you sell a product that is fulfilled via a warehouse, can be sent via UPS, or is a coupon that can be used to purchase goods and services in the real world, you are running a commerce company.

What's important is to begin: build your site, build your traffic, then continue to shape and evolve your business concept. Equally important, remember that what you are presenting to the public is credibility, and your goal is to develop trust in your audience. The more authentic you are perceived by your audience, the more sincere and credible, the more likely it is they will trust you and be willing to buy products or services from you.

Leverage off the Giants

It makes a lot of sense on the Net, to leverage off the giants. Sites such as Google and Amazon are well-established and have spent many millions or billions of dollars to develop technology, infrastructure, marketing, and a brand name. They are product and/or advertising "factories" that make it relatively simple for you to sell their products, if you develop a website that attracts a specific demographic and will serve as a "front door" to their online showrooms.

All you have to do is nurture a specific niche, hone your website and presentation, develop interesting, valuable content that speaks to your audience, and then put up the ads or product widgets leading to landing pages that the giants have so painstakingly developed to showcase their wares.

Start to Monetize

Google AdSense + Other Advertisers

It's a simple, quick process to sign up for Google AdSense ads payper-click, PPC, model, put up the code snippet on your site, and you, potentially, could be making money on your first day. Granted, it might not be much on the first day or the first month. You will have to build your site, its content, and your traffic. Ad placement is also important and can make a huge difference in your income: see Google's "heat map" for placement tips. Depending on the size of your site, and the value your users find in your authority on a particular subject, Google AdSense ultimately could bring in a few hundred to a few thousand dollars a month or even more.

I increased my Google ad revenues from several hundred to more than $7,000 a month on one site. But Google AdSense, like Google algorithms, can be notoriously fickle and make breathtaking dips overnight, so, the safest course is not to depend on Google AdSense as the main income for your site, but only a nice extra, when the money is good. The bottom line is that you need to develop your own unique product or service, which is not so vulnerable to the vagaries of the Net.

Job Boards

Job boards are an "evergreen" product on the web, not subject to the unpredictable "cardiac arrests" of fads: people will always need jobs. Companies will always need workers, and as they move to more automation, they will need programmers and techs to control and oversee that automation. I decided in my first days on the Net to go for a job board model because of its relative stability, and because it is based on software, not hard-goods suppliers.

There are a number of Job Boards with affiliate programs out there, including several giants, such as CareerBuilder.com and Monster.com. You can compare their affiliate commission structure. Smaller job boards may pay more. For example, Job Thread offers a solution for every budget.

You don't need any tech expertise, as everything is hosted. You probably can develop extra revenue from one site, if you can align a career search with the theme of your site. This is a highly competitive field, however, so you need some kind of unique selling point (USP) to make substantial revenues.

Niche Job Boards

You can also look for a niche job board, where there is less competition and possibly more revenue for you in a well-targeted niche. You might try Googling and browsing through a list of niche job boards to see if any would work well with your site.

Private Label Your Own Job Board

Or you can consider private labeling your own job board, using your branding and targeting your demographic, but utilizing the career expertise, back-end technology, and customer support of a "white label" job board provider. That's what I did for many years: I developed the content and gathered the target demographic and outsourced the technical back end to a job board provider, Job Target, in exchange for a revenue share. My primary role was to address critical issues and develop meaningful content for the professional women and diversity community. I continued to increase my communication and alliances with them, through real world meetings and conferences, such as those hosted by the White House and the Secretary of State in Washington D.C., through **American Educational Research Association (AERA), actually an international organization, and through social media such as Linkedin, Twitter and Facebook.** My ongoing relations and collaboration with these groups helped strengthen the job boards and draw traffic and loyal followers to them. Our groundbreaking Journal, Advancing Women in Leadership, AWL, the first online journal on women's issues, created strong and ongoing research and academic alliances. As a result, AdvancingWomen. com had large followings from top universities in the forefront of diversity and inclusion and prestigious tech feeder universities such as California Polytechnic State University and the Wyss Institute at Harvard. During that time, Job Target provided all the back-end work in exchange for a percentage of each sale. By selecting a "white label" job board provider I was still in charge, and not ceding all the decision making to a faceless big brother. There was a simple control panel where I could manage pricing and packages or bundles, offer other products, and check stats or revenue.

That worked well for a long while. However, change is one constant on the Net. And, if you don't keep up, you fall behind. Ultimately, I felt I had to take back complete control of my job board.

As I began to get ever larger customers, global companies, many of them were the largest in the world, Job Target's customer service didn't keep pace, at least at the level of service I felt my customers expected and required. Job Target's software was not keeping pace and their mobile was tortuously slow out of the gate, at a time when the whole online world had turned to mobile. I had to make a decision.

I did a top to bottom review and went over my client list very thoroughly. I realized I had a number of large global companies particularly in the **engineering, manufacturing and construction industries as well as technology, biotech, medical, financial, government and the defense/security industry.** These are the industries most challenged in diversity hiring. The 80/20 rule applies here, too. 80 percent of the revenue was generated by 20 percent of the clients. I also had a very large base of university clients, some who were leaders in diversity hiring and inclusion; others who were leaders in technology and science.

I knew, from long experience, that making a major change like this, putting in place all the back end software, marketing, technology and management was going to be an "inflection point" in my business, a time when I would have to abandon my 80/20 time rule, if only temporarily, and dive head first into the ararduous process of tackling major change and a disruption of the current processes. I started out by convincing Job Target to release me from my present contract. It was not an easy sell, but one worth doing. I maintained that if they didn't agree, I could leave for cause, but that dissension wouldn't serve either of us well. In the end, we agreed to disagree: they released me from the remaining time on my contract, terming it a "buy out". I really didn't care what they called it, and if that was a face saving gesture for them, and it achieved my goal, then it worked for me as well. I tried to be critical of software and processes but very complimentary and diplomatic about people, the roles they played and the relationship we had. That resulted in an amicable parting, which is what I wanted. It would be a time of creative destruction, dismantling one system, that had worked well for many years, only to become outdated, and finding the right team to help me put together a new system, a technical back end geared to the contemporary day's Net: nimble, with fast, automated but personal customer service, and a vastly increased emphasis on social media outreach and sharing.

I knew from the business coming in that I could increase my revenue multiple times, by honing in again on the 80/20 rule, just focusing on the types of core clients that provide 80% of the revenue but giving more personalized service and vastly improved technology and outreach. I would support global businesses and top universities in meeting their diversity, inclusion and tech hiring goals. I would oversee the best techs whom I had long relationships and knew I could rely on.

As it happened, on just about the same day I stopped doing business with Job Target, it ceased to exist, at least as an independent entity, and was acquired by YourMembership.com, backed by a private equity firm, that would bring more resources to the table. Evidently I was not the only one who noticed Job Target could use a fresh infusion of talent, energy and cash to restore their luster and, hopefully, bring them right back up to speed and on to the next level.

That was history now. I had set a new course for my own business. For about three months I threw myself into identifying and putting together the team to identify and execute the tasks necessary to create a new job board from the ground up. I made certain the concept, design elements and software had all the best practice elements of a state of the art contemporary job board. I also made certain it was designed in a way that, when completed, I could manage it all with relative simplicity, and return to my 80/20 rule. I just had to use judicious out sourcing and software to manage some of the tech back-end pieces of it. And I put an increased focus on reaching out through my job boards and social media to the crème de la crème of professional women, diversity and tech candidates to fill these highly desirable, plum slots in some of the world's largest, best established and most profitable companies.

Here's what my job board, Careers.AdvancingWomen.com looked like.

Corporate recruiting clients have included TMP Worldwide, Sun Microsystems, US Department of Commerce, National Association of Women Lawyers, CareerBuilder.com, FedEx Kinko's, Accenture Technology Solutions, and Guidance Software.

Careers.AdvancingWomen had graphics and pages that funnel a targeted reader, either a job seeker or an employer needing to fill positions or meet federal compliance guidelines for diversity hiring, to my job board, These were pages where I spelled out, in detail, the benefits of my job board. Personally, I am more comfortable with an educational approach, spelling out the specific benefits, rather than having a lot of hype.

Overview – About Our Job Boards
Benefits of Using Our Multi-Channel Approach for Your Job Exposure Diversity Job Candidates Improve Your Bottom Line | Advantages of Niche Job Boards

The goal is to get your target demographic to your main landing page for your product or service, where they can "take a bite out of the apple," to see, specifically, what you are offering them:

Jobs.AllTopTechTalent

I also developed a tech following from one of my blogs, segmented Twitter accounts, @gretchenglas, about tech news, Web Biz, and social media. Because I had that demographic and continuously developed content around those subjects, I also launched a tech job board, Jobs.AllTopTechTalent, that identified hard-to-find tech talent: coders, programmers and developers, network and database administrators. Not only in the nation's largest urban tech centers, but a multitude of businesses located outside of California, New York and D.C, the District of Columbia, including my own city, San Antonio, find the competition very stiff to attract talented techs. We wanted to meet the needs of both employers and job seekers by providing this service for the tech community.

Digital Products

The easiest and most profitable item to sell from the Net is a digital product. This is because, in many cases, the cost to produce is almost zero and the cost to deliver is zero. That is very low overhead. Plus your customers can buy on impulse and get delivery almost immediately. Equally important, you get paid immediately.

Sidestepping the subject of software, the easiest digital item for you to produce to sell is content in the form of an ebook, a Kindle book or PDF, a white paper or audio download.

You can plan your blog posts so that 10 of them can be put together in an ebook. You can compile your blog posts into white papers to be given away, or distributed as an incentive to sign up for your newsletter and offers. Or you can convert them into an ebook that produces revenue for you. **You can sell them from your own site, using a digital delivery system, such as Easy Digital Downloads, or free WordPress plugins that can be used with PayPal.** Or you can convert your content into a Kindle book. Amazon offers a free book to walk you through the process: Building Your Book for Kindle by Kindle Direct Publishing.

There are about 200 million visitors to Amazon every month, and Amazon sells hundreds of items per second, although owner Jeff Bezos is not telling the exact number. The Kindle ebook store is the epicenter of ebook activity, so, if you've targeted your demographic well, there definitely is a market for your information and your book. It may not be a major revenue producer, but , particularly if you boost it through social media, it can raise your profile, increase your credibility and add to your ability to create revenue with other products and services. You can interview celebrities in your field, put up a podcast on your site, and sell it as an audio download. (For a step-by-step tutorial on how to start podcasting, using all free tools to begin, go to Learn How to Podcast 101).

You can create "how-to" videos. You can actually make a video just using your iPhone. If it offers values to your users, you can sell it the same way, via a download.

Affiliate Marketing

A Fast and Easy Way to Start Selling on the Net

If you haven't developed your own product or service, marketing other companies' product or service through affiliate marketing is a viable option. As mentioned, automation is the key to operating a successful website and also to developing passive income. Affiliate sales programs are a great support for passive income because they do a great deal of the heavy lifting for you: creation and fine tuning of the product, marketing, sales pitch, payment and fulfillment. All you have to do is attract an audience in your target demographic, identify a product that you believe offers real value to them, and then explain to your audience what the key benefits of that product are.

The best advice, I think, is to first consider carefully what will appeal to your niche. Then focus on a few select products to begin, so you can do them justice and give them adequate promotion.

You will build quality content and product reviews that point to the product or service you are promoting as an affiliate marketer. When one of your readers clicks through and actually purchases a product or service, you get a commission, usually paid out once a month.

The first step is to figure out a profitable niche, remembering that, particularly when you begin, you will be depending on Google search for most of your traffic. In order to see if people are looking for a certain product, open a free Google Adwords account so you can go to the Google Keyword Planner https://adwords.google.com/KeywordPlanner.

You might start by picking a particular product or service and then researching keywords on the Google Keyword Planner to see how many people are looking for that product.

One possibility is to use the Amazon platform with its thousands of products to act as a sales and fulfill back end to your niche site. Amazon doesn't offer the largest commissions because it operates on a razor-thin margin, but it does give a lot of value to your customer. Amazon pays a 4–8 percent commission, so logic would dictate that one would need to select the most expensive items in order to maximize your revenues. However, that is not necessarily the case.

If you succeed in bringing a user to Amazon's site, you will earn a commission regardless of which item they eventually buy. AdvancingWomen, with a theme of careers and business has earned revenue on hundreds of items on Amazon that were not advertised on my site: jewelry, camera, and equipment— all of which my users bought after clicking on a link to Amazon and continuing to browse.

I like to showcase books, because they also serve as new content for the user, keeping her up-to-date on what new books are out there, what's topical, and what's in demand.

If you think books would work for your site's demographic, and you wish to promote a particular book (or series of books) on your website topic, you can do so by becoming an Amazon affiliate. Then you can look through the Kindle Best Seller List to see what's already selling. You can also work with Aer.io, affiliated with Ingram Content Group, a juggernaut in the behind the scenes book publishing, distribution and fulfillment industry, to help promote and market your book, or even help set up your own digital library to sell from.

My business and career content was well-suited to how-to, memoirs, biographies, or topical books about business, all good candidates for promotion to my demographic.

Let's say, for example, I want to promote a book by Michael Lewis, a best selling business author with a big following. I can quickly determine that his book, *Flash Boys: A Wall Street Revolt* was a bestseller. I can also view exactly what its current ranking is.

Test 1

Does the first book in the category have a sales rank less than or equal to 25,000?

Go to the Amazon page for *Flash Boys: A Wall Street Revolt* and view the product details. You can see, in the information below, that, at one time, the book ranked 6 in book sales. That made it a good candidate for you to link to on your site, using an affiliate link, if you have a target demographic that will find value in this book.

First, you would need to go to Amazon and sign up as an affiliate. Then go to the affiliate product and link site and select a test, image, widget, slide show, or other type of link, such as an "a Store," which Amazon will provide for you. All the work is done for you. You just have to select the type of link you want, click on the code that Amazon provides for you, copy it, and then paste it on a sidebar on your site or a page devoted specifically to promoting books on that topic. You can then write a review, or a series of reviews, that points to that link. If a person is visiting your website, your opinion should carry some weight, far more than just putting up an image and link to that product and leaving a reader on his own to figure out if the book is something he might like and should explore further.

Many Affiliate Options

You can also review the offers at ClickBank and CJ Affiliate by Conversant, formerly Commission Junction and review products' earnings and commission structure to determine if a product might be a good fit with your site.

A five-star reviewed, rated, free book on Amazon is Affiliate Marketing 101: Book 4 of the Make Money Online

Entrepreneur Series [Kindle Edition] by Kip Piper (author). This book spells out all the details of going the affiliate route.

Finding a Product to Sell Online

There are many ways to find a product to sell online. The best suggestion again, is to stick to your niche and identify something that offers a real value to your customers.

You can find a product to resell or to private label. You can also have a product manufactured for you, or, if you have that kind of talent, you can invent something to sell. This is a challenging process because you don't want to put something out on the market and have a competitor, who is hungrier or greedier, duplicate what you are selling and undercut you on price.

For a comprehensive look at the most conceivable ways to come up with a suitable product, Timothy Ferriss' book, *The 4-Hour Work week,* goes into great detail about the wide range of resources and possibilities available. See "Step III: A is for Automation, Chapter 9, Income Autopilot I: Finding the Muse," his word for a low maintenance, sustainable business.

Don't Marry It, Test It

You first must identify a profitable product with a relatively generous commission. It must align with the goals and personality of your website in order for it to sell in sufficient volume to generate substantial profits for you. Just because a product flies out the virtual door on someone else's site, don't assume it will sell on yours. Your product has to fit in with your overall expertise and what your site is about in order for people to go there and look for it, much less buy it. Even if a product fits your site and its personality like a hand in a glove, don't assume it will sell. The pricing might not be right; the market might be saturated; and the stars might not line up right. Who knows why some things sell on any particular site and others don't? You can't be clairvoyant: you're not a mind reader, you're a web marketer. Everyone has 20/20 hindsight.

There's a simple way to figure this out. The best plan is first to research what is selling on other sites, such as eBay, Amazon, and Alibaba and figure out which products have a healthy profit margin or affiliate percentage pay out. Then just put up a product and test it out. It either sells or it doesn't. Sometimes you can tweak it—tweak the price, tweak the offer. But often people just aren't interested in buying that product from your site and that's all you really need to know.

Whether you wish to sell ads related to your content, join an affiliate marketing program, sell your own products on your site, or supplement those sales with sales on Amazon or eBay, there are a lot of moving parts to get right on a website and you will need to make a lot of good choices along the way. The way to do this is by testing: testing ad placement and color, testing content, testing product categories, testing various suppliers and vendors, testing affiliate marketing programs to see which ones work for you. Google has an entire "heat map" showing the best placement of ads. It can even suggest the best colors.

Those who take the time to test everything they are doing and act on those tests are the ones who eventually become successful in whichever field they choose.

I can't begin to tell you how many things I've tested. I've tested many, many products that "failed to launch" and weren't promising enough to be developed further. Even in the three core revenue producers on the AdvancingWomen.com site (employment recruiting, advertising, and website production), I've been through a dozen morphing and transfiguration experiments, starting with Double Click ads, from the day they were born, to some new European ad company that sweet talked me into believing it was going to take the Net by storm, but all it did was truly anemic revenues and gave me one more learning experience. All this was before I morphed my way into a successful combination of Google ads, text ads sold from my site, and some proprietary ad networks. It just took time and testing.

It's the same with a job board or employment recruiting facet of Careers. AdvancingWomen.com. I was a part of every one of what seemed like a half dozen permutations of what eventually became CareerBuilder.com. All of them made a small amount of money, from $300 on up. But I didn't get into the thousands of dollars until I started my own job board, with my own branding.

Building Websites

Building automated business websites was something I got into when customers, with no urging from me, requested I help them out with building their websites. That part of the business was dubbed GG Web Group, which has created websites and executed social media marketing for national organizations, universities, green businesses, European software companies, and political organizations. My goal was always aligned with whatever their goal was: sometimes it was increasing revenues; sometimes it was increasing traffic to their sites or exposure to a particular community, possibly global. Always, it was to craft their business so they ran as efficiently as possible with key tasks accomplished by digital automation.

My clients have had website traffic that jumped 400 percent in a week. My prices and services ranged from a **free 15-minute introductory phone call** to the less expensive, at the time:

- Website Services, Consultation $125 per hour

- SEO Website Review, Email Report, 30-Minute Phone Call—$250 total, for the review, the report, and the telephone conference
- Advanced, Technical or Larger website—$3,250 to as much as $8,000, depending on the size and complexity.

Soon the workload grew to a point that it involved a considerable degree of outsourcing. I found that you might have to "kiss a lot of frogs' ' before you found your "prince" in outsourcing. Eventually, I put together a team of talented specialists: designers, technologists, and programmers with numerous certifications attesting to their capabilities to deliver business value and improve the quality of the websites of customers with whom we dealt. However, I can attest that I might have to try a half dozen or more providers before I found one I was truly satisfied with, even more to find a provider I wanted to work with day in and day out. I mean that literally, because, at the time, working in 6 to 12 different time zones, it *was* day in and day out.

There were some companies that asked me to serve on the board for $8,000, as well as work with their public outreach and communications staff. One notable company wanted me to oversee all its business processes, digital public relations, and other communications, for a substantial salary, in addition to constructing its website for a separate fee.

The good news was that by using outsourcing and by using different teams with different specialties, I could manage a project by breaking it down into components and oversee different teams working on each individual component simultaneously. That gave me great elasticity in being able to ramp up the number and type of experts needed to work on various sites at the same time. That method also made for a rapid ramp up in the site's quality, traffic, and results.

However, even though I was outsourcing most of the execution, I was working with different stakeholders and sometimes even different stakeholders within the same company. I was still responsible for helping to form and execute the vision of the website owner, for quality control and project management. In the end, I had to remind myself that a service is a great deal more labor intensive than a product. I decided to scale back any actual web development and convert what I knew about creating websites and communities on the web into a product, which has become this book. This is a less time intensive way, so I can share my passion about creating websites and communities with others. For a time, I continued to do some consulting and reviews of websites. I firmly believe everyone needs an online platform to broadcast the benefits of either their business or their professional skills and, of course, if possible, to provide an extra revenue stream.

Product

There are also many other product testing examples. All you have to do is find the right niche product that resonates with the core target demographic you are building on your site. You must also have a reliable supply, quality control, and the right profit margin that works for you, after all expenses are paid.

So, the best advice is probably to use your common sense to figure out what would be a good product or service for your site to offer. Don't spend an excessive amount of time trying to ponder all the variables. Just put it up. If it makes money, keep it; if it doesn't, drop it. That's the benefit of testing. Oh, and if it makes money, expand it. That's the road to success.

If you've already launched and aren't seeing the results you were hoping for, stop, take a deep breath, and start thinking seriously about your business model and your revenue stream(s). Ask yourself if your assumptions are panning out. Once you have your website up, you have a built-in, real-world, focus group. You have to ask the hard questions. Does your basic product or service generate enough revenue? Or do you think the revenue has the potential to grow sufficiently to sustain you?

This is really a threshold question, as you can't plan, launch, and operate a business with no money. You can probably get it launched, but there are still associated costs. You can devote 100 percent of your time to it and get by on minimal costs for a while , but, eventually, you have to make a living. You can hold down a daytime job and work on this business in the evenings and on weekends, but still, eventually, your business or career website has to sustain itself, so this is a question you should face and resolve sooner rather than later.

If what you're doing now isn't working, change it. Ask for help. Get yourself on the right track.

For example, I was working with a young colleague, a grad student programmer at San Francisco University on an app he wanted to develop. It was to be a "handsfree" study app using voice recognition, which was not as common in those days, shortly before iPhone's Siri came on the scene. He was stuck trying to use a program called "Open Ears," the most popular shared-source iOS framework for speech recognition and text-to-speech on the iPhone and iPad.

Open Ears was not fully functional in the app, with no continuous playback, which was critical. I developed a couple of options about how to proceed, one of which was to hire a guru to execute that piece of the software. I quickly came upon Halle Winkler, founder of Politepix UG (haftungsbeschränkt), iOS designer, and developer in Berlin, Germany. Halle, it turns out, had created and launched OpenEars, and all its subsidiary products. So Halle was not simply a tech guru. She was The Guru for Open Ears.

I connected to Halle on LinkedIn—at the time, we had about 18 LinkedIn connections in common. I provided my LinkedIn profile, described the problem and asked for an estimate from her to do the work. She graciously offered to Skype with my tech colleague, to see if it wasn't some minor tech glitch that she could talk him around in a few minutes. And that's ultimately what happened. They Skyped, she told him how to solve the OpenEars problem, and we moved on from there. That's one reason I love the Net. There's often camaraderie and a desire to help you from others who consider you one of them.

My point is that help is out there if you ask for it. Sometimes what seems like an insurmountable problem to you or me, can be a simple two-minute instruction for a real expert in that specialized area.

It also reminds me of a woman tech who helped me when I was just getting started on the Net and was struggling to master HTML. I came across some coding that I just couldn't do, no matter how much I researched it. At the time, there was a women's tech group called Webgrrls in Silicon Valley, and one of them leaped into my dilemma—she was a women's advocate as well—and said "I'm going to help you with this." She and her tech friends were my tech mentors and support for a full two years, as I fumblingly developed my own skills and work methods. I eventually had the pleasure of meeting her in person in San Francisco. Her name was Roan Bear, and I still think of her as a guardian angel, without whom I might never have been able to ramp up AdvancingWomen and also my other initiatives.

So, if you need help, ask for it. You can't imagine what kinds of doors it might open for you.

CHAPTER 4

CREATE YOUR WEBSITE

BAKE IN AUTOMATION

Again, start with the basics. You are going to need:

- A web host
- A domain

IPage.com and Bluehost.com are both services I have used; both are highly rated and reliable and both offer web hosting starting at less than $5 a month. When you sign up for a web host, you can purchase your domain name at the same host. IPage.com and BlueHost.com, as well as many other web hosts, offer one-click installation of WordPress and simple control panels to run your site.

Which Website Software to Use

WordPress has revolutionized ordinary people's ability to rapidly deploy an attractive, sophisticated website, which can then be updated in plain text.

According to Wikipedia, "WordPress is a free, open source Content Management System (CMS), often used as a blog publishing application, powered by PHP and MySQL.

It has many features including plugin architecture and a template system. WordPress is the most popular CMS in use today." Being open source, it has thousands of donated staff hours of coding and is constantly being refreshed and updated by expert coders.

It is powerful and elegant, plus it offers many plugins and widgets, automated pieces of software, which work in the background doing essential tasks that it used to take programmers many hours to do. These tasks include search engine optimization, providing Google with a sitemap and a constant stream of updates, and a thousand more functions, all of which work together, automatically in the background, to make your site a success.

If you want to build your own brand, you will need a standalone platform, one which does not require you to use its company name as part of the URL, such as Blogger.com/yourname. WordPress is the leading platform and, as its website points out, "It comes in two flavors: the fully hosted WordPress.com, and the self-hosted version available at WordPress.org."

You should opt for WordPress.org, so you can begin establishing your own identity and brand. It is feature rich, continuously updated, with thousands of hours in development time. It boasts communities of developers offering plugins that automate hundreds of the most useful tasks imaginable, from search engine optimization (SEO), so your blog can be found, to spam catching, to putting in GoogleAdSense or Yahoo ads on every post. New plugins are offered almost daily and there is ample support for whatever your needs are. There are many ways to customize the plugins, widgets, and themes or change them with a single click. And did I mention, it's free?

Once you have installed your WordPress.org blog, you will have to familiarize yourself with how to use it. Although we know there are bloggers galore on every topic imaginable out there, we understand that you might be stopped cold at the thought of starting a blog. You might like to, but it seems too complex, too involved, too frustrating, too ... whatever.

To those of us who've already taken the high dive off the cliff and into the warm and welcoming waters of the blogosphere, the whole process now seems rather user friendly and simple. We perhaps forget where we started—a totally blank slate on the subject. Or, as we've discussed, zero domain expertise. That's exactly where I started.

I remember the first time I looked at the admin side of a WordPress page, with no training and no preparation. I thought, *What on earth is this and how am I supposed to learn it?* (I think mild panic sets in at the first glance of the unknown, particularly when we know we're supposed to *do* something with it—like produce a published page, but how do you do that?). I was on my own. This book is an attempt to make the process easier for all the hopeful bloggers out there. Think of a blog post as a conversation between you and the reader. You just want to share what you know with someone else in a few clear, creative, and engaging words. Let's see if we can break this down into bite-size pieces.

Getting Started with WordPress Tutorials

When you sit down, shake off that little twinge of "beginner's anxiety," and start to use it, WordPress has extremely intuitive administration. You will be able to compose a post and publish it on your website with just one click!

WordPress.org offers its own Quick Start Guide, which, incidentally, points out the advantages of self hosting. It's pretty straightforward and intuitive. If you prefer to use a video go to this site:

WordPress Overview

- How to Login to WP Dashboard

- How to Write a Post
- How to Write a Page
- How to Edit Posts/Pages
- How Widgets Work
- How to Moderate Comments
- WordPress Settings Overview
- How to Upgrade WordPress Using the Automatic Plugin
- How to Add new Users
- How to Change/Activate Themes

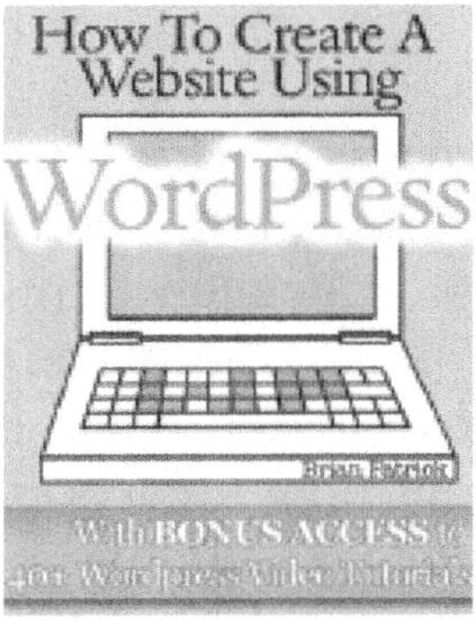

If you prefer, you can also download a free book from Amazon, walking you through the process of building a WordPress website.

Themes, Essential Content, and Links

As for design, WordPress has a huge array of free themes you can select. Because your goal is to achieve your website objectives with as little wasted time, effort, and energy as possible, using a WordPress theme definitely is a good choice. You will get an attractive, professionally designed and coded, search engine optimized platform for your site, at the click of a mouse, which you can then customize to reflect you and the topic of your website.

You should use a theme which is "responsive"—that is, one that will display optimally on any device, whether desktop, iPad, or Smartphone. The theme will be labeled "responsive" if it has that capability. With the huge trend toward the mobile web, using a responsive theme is a must. WordPress offers a number of free responsive themes. I have used Twenty Thirteen, which now has an update to Twenty Fourteen.

WordPress offers a lot of themes for many different types of websites, so take a look around and see which ones seem to suit you. Don't get too stressed about it, because you can always change it with the click of a mouse. You just want to try it, see how it works, and if it doesn't work for you, or you come across one that works better, then move on.

Here's how the process works. On the WordPress admin control panel, in the left column, look for "Appearance," and under that, "Themes." Click on "Themes" and WordPress will take you to the page where your existing themes are loaded. You can click to activate one and you can also click to get a live preview of how a certain theme would appear on your site, although you might have to tweak how the Navigation Bar at the top looks. You can also search for and upload other new themes.

There are different levels of themes from the simple to the complex. I suggest that you start with a simple theme. In other words, deploy the "KISS" theory of Keep It Simple. That way, you can get the feel of WordPress, learn how to use it, and put your own stamp of originality on it: your content, the images you choose, your perspective, so that it really reflects who you are and what you are trying to convey to your users in order for them to be tempted to buy the service or product your site offers. It will be a lot easier to start and get this accomplished with a simple theme template. Later, if you like, move up to a more complex theme. Although it is a great bonus to have a super attractive website, remember that acquiring users and ultimately customers will always come down to your credibility and the quality of the product or service you are offering. Consider this example of the largest dating site in the world, not known for its design, or should I say, not known for its good design.

In 2009, *Inc.* magazine featured an article, titled "And the Money Comes Rolling In" (http://www.inc.com/magazine/20090101/and-the-money-comesrolling-in.html). "Markus Frind works one hour a day and brings in $10 million a year. How does he do it? He keeps things simple."

Frind, founder and CEO of Plenty of Fish, the world's largest dating website, is basically a demon coder. He doesn't much care about the rest as he doesn't believe it affects his bottom line. As the 2009 *Inc.* article points out,

> Plenty of Fish is a designer's nightmare; at once minimalist and inelegant, it looks like something your nephew could have made in an afternoon. There's the color scheme that seems cribbed from a high school yearbook and the curious fondness for **bold** text and CAPITAL LETTERS. When searching for a prospective mate, one is inundated with pictures that are not cropped or properly resized. Instead, headshots are either comically squished or creepily elongated, a carnivalesque effect that makes it difficult to quickly size up potential mates.
>
> Frind is aware of his site's flaws but isn't eager to fix them ... Fixing the wonky images, for instance, might actually hurt Plenty of Fish. Right now, users are compelled to click on people's profiles in order to get to the next screen and view proper headshots. That causes people to view more profiles and allows Frind, who gets paid by the page view, to serve more

ads. "The site works," he says. "Why should I change what works?"

At the time, more than 50 million registered users visited Plenty of Fish more than 430 million times each month. But the brilliance of Plenty of Fish was not its strength as a matching engine; it was the site's low overhead. Frind managed to run his company with almost no staff. However, after that rocket start propelled his success, Frind decided to ramp up his staff and improve the look of his website and it is still paying off.

This is what Plenty of Fish, or POF, looks like today:

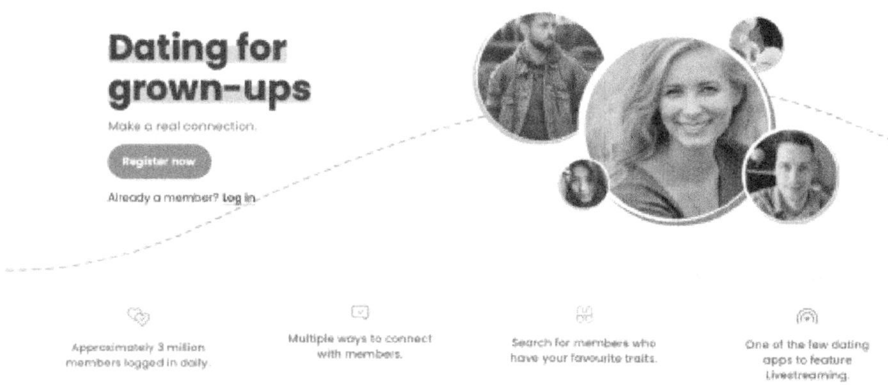

What the site offers—virtual dating matchups—and its efficiency in producing them on a large scale, provides a real value to its users.

So the lesson is—not to go out and start a dating site, particularly if you don't have the programming chops to churn out hyper efficient and competitive code— but to focus on providing the customer a real value, in the form of the products or the services you offer.

There is a hierarchy of theme template complexity, although not necessarily effectiveness. Free WordPress themes might be considered the entry level, but there's no reason you can't continue using them, if they accomplish your goals, which are to generate traffic and revenue.

There are thousands of specific WordPress themes and WordPress e-commerce themes available. These range from WP e-Commerce, a free download, to WooCommerce "WooCommerce can be downloaded for free, with extensions available for purchase. WooCommerce features include sales reports, control over shipping and tax charges, a customer account area, order management, product and inventory management, coupon codes, and more."

You can pick WordPress themes or you can step it up a notch and get more of the work and behind-the-scenes maintenance done for you. See 40+ of the Best WordPress eCommerce Themes).

Shopify powers more than visited by 100K+ users in the past month, used as a sales platform by 1,000,000 businesses. You can get started today, choose from multiple templates, get a marketing and SEO and a payment system, sell online, at your retail store, or on mobile. There's an inexpensive starter setup and free trials for more expensive packages.

There are also hundreds of premium themes for which you pay a relatively small price—most designed for a specific type of website. You can find premium themes for every type of business from automotive, city guides, daily deals, lawyers, restaurants, selling ebooks, spas, travel, and vacation rentals, for example. You name it, you can find it and multiple versions of it on the different premium theme sites. Here is a link to WordPress Premium Themes Directory, http://www.premiumwp.com/premium-wordpress-themes-directory/.

Here are a couple of contrasting examples of professional theme templates you can customize, the first from Templatic.com:

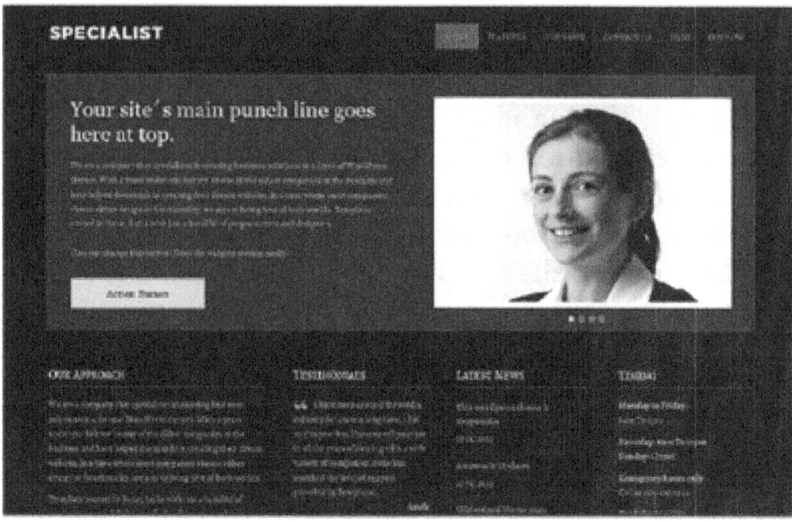

As the StudioPress site states,

MomPreneur is a fun, but professional and functional feminine WordPress theme ideal for women business owners. The premium theme is designed to combine your business website with a blog and a shop thanks to full ecom merce integration. It utilises the WooCommerce ecommerce plugin so you can easily set up an online store to sell whatever you want. MomPreneur includes 3 different colour styles, 2 layout options, custom background, menus and header, theme options, and social media icons. It also has a responsive design so adapts to work perfectly on all mobile devices including iPhones and iPads. MomPreneur is a premium child theme for the excellent Genesis Framework and is available in the StudioPress Community Marketplace.

Genesis is an advanced and well-coded framework used by a lot of professionals. A lot of professionals also use the Thesis theme, because it is simple, elegant and endlessly customizable without having to code. Thesis is, right off the bat, an expertly-coded framework. Thesis, like Genesis, is known for the quality of its design and search engine optimization, SEO, which is critical because it is SEO traffic that drives a large part of the success of a website. There are also many free or inexpensive "skins" (or looks) available that overlay the Thesis framework, including responsive skins, which you will definitely want. You will have any number of options to choose from. But to keep it simple, and for your own look, go to Istockphoto.com, or one of the other stock graphic sites, put in your keywords to search for suitable photos, pay anywhere from nothing to a few dollars for a half dozen photos and then you're almost ready to go.

All the options, above the entry-level, free WordPress themes, might have more coding built in for the specific type of business they are targeting, but they might require some expert help to get set up properly. Also, even if you get tech help setting it up, you have to know what you want to include, and that might require some expertise and experience you only can acquire over time.

I definitely would wait until I had more experience and familiarity with the WordPress platform before attempting to move up to these more complex themes. If you fall deeply in love with one of these premium themes, you are, of course, free to go for it. You should be prepared to get assistance from a freelance tech at a freelance platform like Upwork and spend a good deal of time explaining what you want, and getting together the "digital assets" or photos, videos, and content, to flesh out the theme's framework.

Also, you should be aware that styles continue to change and evolve on the Net. Just as the type of website that populated the Net a few years ago has changed, so have some of the concepts for design. This is often due to technical advances, such as those required by the advent of the mobile web, or the evolution of ecommerce, or the continuing refinement and specialization of websites themselves.

The death knell has been tolled for some of these as reported in "Goodbye to 8 Design Elements Whose Time Has Come." Of these, the ones you need to be aware of are the following:

> **1. The Drop-Down Menu**
>
> Drop-down menus have been a cornerstone of user interfaces since the dawn of the Internet. Countless sites continue to use hover state drop-down lists as a critical piece of navigation, but as trends shift toward fully responsive, device-agnostic design, there won't continue to be simple drop-down menus.
>
> In its current form, the drop-down menu cannot function on platforms where the concept of a "hover state" doesn't exist (on tablets and phones). As the "mobile first" movement continues gaining traction,

click-based navigation, such as the use of a "hamburger button" to nest an entire site's navigation in a clickable list, will become more prevalent.

2. Carousel

The carousel is another ancient relic (by Internet standards, at least) of web UI that enables pages to feature multiple content elements within a certain spot above the fold. Typically set to cycle based on time, carousels have been phased out, particularly on major news sites, in favor of adaptive content blocks that fill space based on browser width. Again, the death of this trend benefits mobile and tablet users, who avoid frustrating experiences attempting to "swipe" through a carousel or navigate between elements. The carousel as we know it will likely evolve into a more gallery-like interface based on swipes and navigation rather than a time-based approach.

You will be hearing a lot about "flat design," that strips away the attempt to mimic three dimensional objects in the real world. And here is the other design element whose time is past

3. Web Pages

Web pages are still around, but they're undergoing some serious innovation lately … We've seen a major shift towards "appification" of web sites … the pageless design with a new-at-the time HTML5 standard called PushState which updated content asynchronously without refreshing the navigational elements of the page

In other words, it pushes the content onto the page you're looking at instead of having to navigate to it. Gawker Media, http://gawker.com, with its 47 million monthly users, along with its gadget site, Gizmodo, was an early adopter of this appification approach. "We will see a greater number of sites take this approach because it makes them leaner, faster, and cheaper to run."

The good news, for you, and much of the rest of the Net, is that these design forecasts by the Net fashion forward techs and design conceptualists take some time, as much as several years, to play out. So, if you have a drop-down menu, for example, you have some lead time, or a "long runway," as Amazon's Jeff Bezos says, to transition to the newer design.

Essential Content and Links

When configuring links on your theme template, be sure to put in an "About Page," a "Contact Page," and a "Landing Page" or other description of your product or service, with complete pricing and a link to a payment method.

Your "About Page" likely will be the second most visited page after your home page. Users will want to know who you are and what your credentials are relative to the topic of your site. Why should they trust you or believe you on this topic? You do not have to be a PhD or a Rhodes scholar. You do not have to have an MBA or have worked for General Motors or Google. You do have to know your subject better than most of your target market. It is also ok if you are enamored of your subject and a perpetual learner about it. Perhaps it's something you've loved since childhood.

Harry and David, http://www.harryanddavid.com, for example, don't need to know about a lot of things. They just need to know how to harvest or procure fresh fruit and gourmet items, and then market and deliver them. As far as the Net is concerned, everything else they know is superfluous. They do have to present themselves, convincingly, as authentic and genuinely concerned about their customers and so do you.

Automate Your Web Biz

Clearly, you don't want your website to *just* be pretty. You want it to work hard for your business, too. In order for that to happen, you've got to install automated functions into your website for it to perform. And you have to tell your website visitors how they should interact with you, if they are interested in your product or service.

By installing plugins and widgets—think of them as little robots keeping your website humming—and putting on autopilot as many small, routine tasks as possible, you will be freed for the big moment, the huge contracts, the momentous decisions.

Plugins

Plugins are the little pieces of code that handle dedicated tasks for you automatically, and they are easy to install. You just click on plugins on the left side panel of your WordPress installation. From there, you will go to the page where your existing plugins are installed, some of which come configured with WordPress. In the search box at the top you put in the keyword or actual name of the plugin you are looking for. When you see it, click install. Installation will be automatic and just about instantaneous. Click "activate," then click "return to the plugin page. Voila! You've added an entire automated task to your website. Here are some examples that I use.

Let's start with a couple of simple tasks.

SEO, Search Engine Optimization

The All in One SEO Pack plugin is specifically designed for search engine optimization. The first task you have is to get your site discovered by the search engines and, to do that well, you have to do everything you can to make it "discoverable." This includes a description and using "keywords" for each page or post you write.

Conscientious use of SEO, along with fresh content daily, is what will get users beating a path to your site. Amy Sandoz, who earns $2,500–$5,000 per month selling emergency kits at Ready Set to Go Kits credits the *SEO for Dummies* book for being "super helpful" in starting her business.

Google XML Sitemap

Sitemaps are a way to tell Google about pages on your site that might not otherwise be discovered. In its simplest terms, an XML Sitemap—usually called Sitemap, with a capital S—is a list of the pages on your website. If you use the plugin, it will keep Google updated.

(When you have completed installing your plugins and widgets, and your site is ready to launch, you will want to submit it to search engines to start the traffic flowing.)

Customer Contact

How will your customer get in contact with you? Don't just give an email address. And certainly don't give an email address that your friends might find cute but your customers will perceive as unprofessional, like snugglybunny@yahoo.com or bigbadbear@hotmail.com. Better to use a contact form where you receive a standardized heading in your inbox, have some control over what information is given, and you can use a captcha device to filter out spam. There are plenty of free contact forms out there and, at least one will , no doubt be offered by your web host.

These contact forms typically can integrate with 20 email marketing and contact management services and automatically sends newsletter subscriber data to third-party apps, such as MailChimp, Constant Contact, Vertical Response, GetResponse, ActiveCampaign, and AWeber. You might also add Donation Forms, Appointment Forms, and Newsletter Forms. You can have it appear on every page or only selected pages.

Some Contact forms offer a number of options, including links to your social media sites, but they do require a little integration. For some uses, you might have to insert a "form key" into a snippet of script—this is like a product key in that it enables the product to work. Although this is a simple copy-and-paste operation, if you are absolutely terrified of a snippet of code or otherwise determined never to touch the stuff, then you should put this off until later, when you're feeling more comfortable with the whole process. You can integrate your Contact forms with AWeber or another email marketing system.

Newsletter Forms will also be hosted from your site. These forms have a somewhat different function, as this is the customer's "opt in," that is required for you to send email and notices to a customer. Not only is getting an opt in the polite, considerate thing to do but, the CAN-SPAM Act, is a **law** that sets the rules for commercial email, establishes requirements for commercial messages, gives recipients the right to have you stop emailing them, and spells out tough penalties for violations. Top email marketing systems are rigorous in adhering to these rules and will want to know where you obtained your lists. Most require a signup directly with them. Newsletter forms have a professional look that will encourage users to opt in. They also offer a range of options and integrate with email marketing systems, including AWeber. See more on this subject at "How to Develop Your Email Lists," later in this chapter

Once one of these plugins is installed, it is a hands-free automated process that really will get the conversation between you and your potential customer off and running.

Spam Catcher / Security

Akismet is a spam-catching plugin that comes configured with WordPress. According to estimates, 52 percent of WordPress users activate Akismet. I highly recommend it, as it's great at catching spam.

Engagement Tools

Related Posts by Zemanta

You can add automatically generated related posts, which you select, in the footer of your content. If they match up with your content, I find these add interest and depth to your page. The example below is from A Tsunami of Mobile Impact Is Coming, Much of It is Already Here

Shareaholic Share Buttons, Analytics, and Related Content

Shareaholic adds share buttons to all the most popular social media to help you identify your most popular posts and pages and help your content go viral, attracting more users.

Comment Systems

WordPress comes with a native comment system. However, the following systems have more robust functionality: Facebook, Disqus, IntenseDebate, and LiveFyre. Each has their distinct strong points. I have used LiveFyre because it has the capability of pulling in comments from posts on your Facebook page and Twitter page and encourages social media discussion

Ad Tools

OIOpublisher Ad Manager

Control your ad space with OIOpublisher. You can use Google AdSense as a default, but allow users to pay for and post their own ads on your side. If the potential advertisers for your target demographic are not tech savvy, or a bit anxious about their tech skills, you can provide an option to help them for a small fee. If you choose to do this, I would accumulate orders and give them once a week to a virtual assistant (like TaskRabbit) to put up for your client. You can pass the charge along.

If you want to explore other ad management options, go to *What are the Best Ad Management Plugins and Solutions for WordPress?*

Tracking

Register for Google Analytics for tracking purposes. This is the de facto standard that others you are dealing with will want to see. If you want a quick overview of your stats, you can install Google Analytics Dashboard for WordPress if you want to display Google Analytics Reports and Real Time Statistics in your dashboard. It also automatically inserts tracking code in every page. However, it's best to review your numbers in detail so you can understand where your traffic is coming from and the content that is gaining the most traction with your users.

I also use Opentracker.Net, an outstanding tracking system from the Netherlands that goes into all kinds of helpful granular detail, such as zip codes, area codes, and every aspect of a website you might be remotely interested in tracking. I use both Google Analytics and Opentracker.Net, as well as BlueHost's own not very robust stat page, but then I'm a bit compulsive about tracking my numbers.

Widget

A widget is a small, standalone snippet of code that also fulfills an automated function. One difference is that plugins work on your site behind the scenes and widgets can be embedded in your website's public face, generally the sidebar. You will find this on the left sidebar under

"Appearance," along with Themes, Headers, and some other items. There are any number of widgets available that will increase your user's engagement and, often, your revenue. Some examples include the following:

Search Widget for WordPress, which you might consider putting at the top of your sidebar to help users navigate your site. You must have a menu that defines the general navigation, but if looking for something particular, a search function is invaluable. Add your Twitter.com or Facebook widget on the sidebar to drive more traffic, or put up affiliate links, such as Amazon, to drive revenue.

Submit to Search Engines

In order to get the traffic flow started to your site, you will have to submit it to search engines. This is really repetitive work, which is already done rapidly and inexpensively by a number of services or freelancers who've developed automated processes to handle that chore. I would recommend using one of them and saving your energies for tasks that only you can do, such as writing or cu rating valuable relevant content. There are people on all the freelance platforms who will do this task for you and report back to you in a few days, Premier, on Fiverr.com for instance, will submit your site to 400 search engines for $5. Then, as inbound traffic starts, install a way to communicate with your potential customers.

How to Develop Your Email Lists

If you want to make money on more than a random basis, the best way to do that is to set up an email capture form for your website, so you can market to "opt-in" subscribers on a regular basis. Again, you want to outsource the rote work. Use one of the robust email marketing platforms, such as AWeber or Newsletter Forms from ContactUs, which will provide templates and do all the simple repetitive tasks for you:

- website signup forms
- auto responders for follow up
- sending emails
- performance tracking

In order to get your users to sign up and start the process of communication, you should offer them something: a newsletter, special offers, or, the most compelling, a free gift, which can be an information product, such as a white paper or PDF about the subject on which you offer your expertise.

Email Platforms

There are a number of email platforms to choose from. But, overall, I would recommend AWeber, and here's why:

MailChimp Vs AWeber Email Marketing—Why I Switched! by Cliff Ravenscraft In this post Cliff Ravenscraft, otherwise known as the Podcast Answer Man, shares how he came to recognize the critical importance an email list plays in sales and how he finally settled on AWeber.

Initially Cliff signed up with MailChimp because it was free. As it turned out MailChimp was only free for the first two months because his list, with the addition of an email service platform grew and exceeded his free limit, which, at the time, was 500. Now it's many multiples of that.

But the fact is, the success of using an email platform to enhance the communication and profitability of his business forced him into taking another hard look at which service offered the best features for him.

> "When I sent out that first message, I had a mere 131 people signed up to the list. The message I sent out was to promote a series of seven online webinars that I was going to perform over a period of six

weeks. These webinars were going to cover the seven topics that people had hired me the most to teach in my one on one consulting sessions. The cost of attending each webinar was $100 and I offered the ability to have access to all seven webinars at the cost of $595.00.

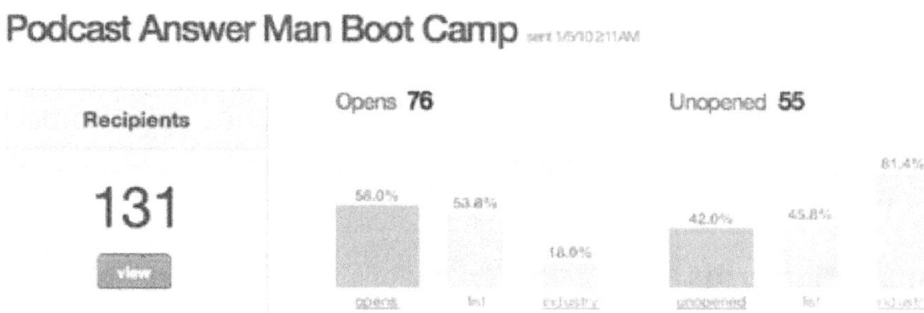

As you can see from the image on page 82, this message went out to all 131 people who had subscribed to my mailing list. Out of those who received the message, 76 of them actually opened the email to read my message. This single email caused me to sell out every one of my available spots in those seven webinars. I used a webinar service with a limit of 15 people at the time. My first email sent to my Podcast Answer Man mailing list generated just over $10,000 of income for my business within six days of sending out that message.

Since that first email, I have had multiple experiences where a single message has generated somewhere between $2,000 to just over $16,000 of income for my business.

I have learned a great deal about the value of building a relationship of trust with an audience who is genuinely interested in what I have to say about a particular topic and offering them the option to sign up for exclusive announcements, via an email list, related to that particular topic.

Simply put, ***there is power in "the list."***
—Quoted with permission of the author, Cliff Ravenscraft.

Cliff goes on to describe what he considers the superior features on AWeber. It is important to remember however that Cliff already had a robust business model developed. So, to begin, you should use an automated email platform to develop your list and grow your business. Then take full advantage of all the templates, features, and automation of the email platform to broadcast the benefits of your offerings and turbocharge your business.

Selling

If you are offering your own products or services, you should **standardize your prices!**

Ideally, you should have firm prices in advance, so each time you have a prospect, you don't have to go through the draining process of facing a whole new set of decisions to establish a price for that particular item. In order to set firm prices, you will have to "systematize" your business; that is, sit down and think through every step that goes into producing the final product or service, how much it costs, then add in your profit margin. Business is rife with owners who forgot to add in the cost of delivery, or didn't calculate the true cost of raw materials, or didn't tack on overhead costs, so that each item they thought they were shipping for a profit, actually turned out to be putting them further in the hole. Here's an example from "6 Common Mistakes People Make When Starting a Business, http://www.entrepreneur.com/article/232240#

Expensive mistake #2: Bad pricing

> "My single biggest mistake with my first business--a handbag company--was in pricing," says Sarah Shaw, CEO of Entreprenette, a consulting firm in Durango, Colo. Hers is a common misstep for product manufacturers.
>
> "I didn't understand that with any kind of clothing or accessories, you have to calculate the square footage

of fabric, including the wasted fabric," Shaw explains. Without an accurate understanding of her costs, she couldn't price her products correctly.

"I thought you sort of doubled everything, but that's not correct," she says. "It's a 2.5-times markup from cost to wholesale, which covers marketing, the showroom fee, and all your expenses."

That business ultimately closed down after 9/11, but entrepreneur Sarah Shaw, in typical entrepreneur fashion, was on to another, this time, hugely successful business, selling cosmetic bags and organizing baskets to more than 400 stores nationwide with exclusive distribution deals in Australia and Japan, raising her profit margin and simplifying her work flow

Sarah Shaw managed to turn lemons into lemonade. You, however, are reading this book so you can avoid lemons: be aware and forewarned about potential pitfalls and one of the biggest of these is bad pricing. Be extra cautious and review all your costs, including overhead costs, like a medical examiner on TV's *CSI* looking for a hidden clue.

When you are absolutely certain you have every cost included, then you can set firm prices on each item you sell. That will allow you to spend your energy figuring out the system, not dealing with improvised solutions to moment-by-moment issues or problems.

Next Step: Link Those Firm Prices to Online Payment Functions

This is simple enough. If you don't already have one, then go to PayPal.com to set up an account so you can take online payments through major credit or debit cards or electronic checks. The small transaction fee is well worth enabling the buyers to act now, online, with whatever method best suits them. You can go into PayPal.com's merchant tools and set up a badge to install on your website that allows a user to choose any of the products or services at the prices you've inputted and also has an option to track your inventory or profit, if you choose, another automated timesaver. You can also use FreshBooks.com to automate much of the estimating, time tracking, and invoicing work. You can al low clients to receive invoices and pay online. You also can put recurring invoices on autopilot and allow clients to pay invoices online through Paypal.com.

Finally, Put a Customer Intake Form on Your Website

You've used your website to broadcast your credentials and your wares, been successful in attracting a customer, then used your web-site for the actual online payment transaction. Now, you can have the same PayPal.com badge, when completed, direct your customer back to a customer intake form. You can use the Fast Secure Contact form, with its multiform feature to create an intake form where the customer will fill in all the preliminary information you need to begin fulfilling the order. For example, if you are selling sofa slipcovers, you would want to know the dimensions of the sofa, the type of fabric, the color and styling, and other details. Just figure out all the details you need in order to save time collecting them from the customer each time you get an order.

At this point, you're ready to start the process of fulfillment. That's a lot of heavy lifting, completed by your savvy and hardworking website automated functions, which, if used to capacity, will become prized members of your virtual "staff."

Of course, if you go the affiliate route you can eliminate all these steps except the contact form as those functions will be taken care of for you automatically by your affiliate site. At that point, your affiliate site, for example Amazon will take over and complete the fulfillment of the order, handle any customer service, give you a complete accounting and pay you, probably once a month.

CHAPTER 5

WHAT DO I SAY?

WHY YOU SHOULD HAVE A BLOG ON YOUR BUSINESS WEBSITE

Even if you're not interested in sharing any personal details of your life, and want to keep things strictly business on your company website, you still should offer a blog. Put your focus on your goals; breakdown each step in the process. Whether you're building a community from scratch, or you're working to grow an existing one, you can use this process to get your community rolling or optimize and leverage what you already have. Your blog should strive to accomplish the following goals:

- Provide fresh content every day, giving users a reason to come back.
- Position yourself as a thought leader in your field.
- Rank higher in the various search engines.
- Build and burnish your brand.

- Improve communication with your community.
- Demonstrate you know how to solve your community's problem.
- Identify and nurture prospects.

First, Consider Your Goal

Yes, you want to attract and engage your audience members, then, hopefully, lead them to explore your product or service. But even more fundamental than this, is gaining the trust of your audience. Trust is key, and it is the most essential element you will need if you want your users to buy from you.

Which elements combine in a synergistic way to create "trust"? If there was a single, surefire answer to this, it would sell at a price equivalent to liquid gold. It is invaluable. It is also elusive and difficult to define.

An author's "voice" is relatively easy to define. According to Wikipedia, "Voice can be thought of in terms of its uniqueness ... As a trumpet has a different voice than a tuba or a violin has a different voice than a viola, so the words of one author have a different sound than the words of another. One author may have a voice that is light and fast paced while another may have a dark voice." What is your voice? And what is a "voice" that engenders trust?

The first element, of what I believe are intertwining or fusing elements, is authenticity. To be drawn in, and become believers or "true fans," your audience must believe you are speaking from an area of deep authenticity, of core beliefs you hold that are important to share with others.

Second, I believe your voice, by which I mean the tone, tenor, and content of all your writing on your site, must convey a genuine desire to help and support your followers, to provide them with something of value that will improve their lives. This can be a small improvement or a life-changing improvement—doesn't matter. The point is, you are on their side, and you wouldn't take their time if you didn't think you could help them.

Three, if you are writing nonfiction with a premise that you can help to solve someone's problems, your voice must be knowledgeable and pragmatic. If you are writing fiction vampire novels for teenagers, then you will need a different voice. But, for the broad market you will be targeting, being accessible, down-to-earth, and knowledgeable is key. You don't want to be the guy or gal they'd like to sit down and have a beer with. You don't want to be the woman they want to accompany on wild, dark vampire fantasies. You want to be the kindly neighbor with whom they'd trust their child. You want to be the one from whom they would trust buying a product, knowing you are on their side and want them to succeed.

What Should Your Content Strategy Be?

- **Blog for your target market. Discover your ideal prospect or customer and blog for him and her. Use your blog to provide valuable content focusing on solving your user's problems.** Encourage comments and feedback and engage in a conversation with your users, so you will understand better the solutions they are seeking. Don't delve into personal details of your life unless they are directly relevant to your business and will be helpful for a client to know, or unless they showcase your expertise.
- **Start the conversation with your audience, and then keep it going**. Ask your users to sign up for your RSS feed or your email subscription so you can reach out to them through another channel. It's all about user engagement and engendering loyalty to your website and, ultimately, converting that loyalty

to purchasing the products or services you are offering.

- **Insert social bookmarking links.** Multiply the impact of a popular blog post by encouraging your users to share a link to it and using the Shareaholic bar to provide an easy and immediate way for a user to pick a social media site to share the link on.
- **Use your blog traffic to generate prospects.** Build relationships with your users, then put in links and calls-to-action to landing pages, like those generated by LeadPages or those you build yourself, where you make a compelling case to purchase your product or service. Users understand you are in business and it's ok to ask for theirs. Give them your expertise in return.

How to Start Blogging

Maybe you haven't started your own blog yet because you're intimidated. Maybe you're just discovering the blogosphere. Whatever the reason, I can almost guarantee there is such an ease, immediacy, and a sense of shared community with those who will be attracted to your subject and come to read your blog, that once you start, you'll be hooked. You will find *you definitely can* blog. Certainly, if you want to start an online business, it will be helpful to share your expertise and your experiences and begin to build a shared community as a launching point for your business.

Once you're at this point, you just have to be able to write in plain English (or French or German or Spanish or whatever language you speak.) Although the program is really intuitive and simple to learn you can return to the Quick Start Guide or Making a WordPress Blog with screenshots, to walk you step by-step through the process of writing your content, saving it, then publishing it to the Net.

Whatever moves you or stirs you, motivates or inspires you, there will be a community of people on the Net who will be interested and wish to share your passion in the subject and the fresh perspective and new information you bring to it. When you fulfill yourself, those of us who share your passion or your interest in a subject are all one step closer to fulfilling ourselves.

So start your blog. The goal is to get you on the Internet, blogging your heart out, sharing all your stories. Remember: You make the path by walking on it.

Writing your content on Word Press. Once you've gotten your feet wet and are comfortable with the program—perhaps a month or two from when you begin—you should probably try to put in greater originality and more of your own thoughts and stories. But to begin, I would suggest the following three support steps for you:

1. **Set up a reader** to scour the Net for materials that interest you and about which you have some comment, thought, or opinion to share.

Blogging takes time. And keeping up with news and other blogs, so you have something to blog about, takes time. So it's highly recommended that you set up a Google reader, or any other kind of reader, to bring blogs or your favorite kind of information and news *to* you, instead of you going out and searching the Net to track it down. (This will also allow you to get more familiar with the blogosphere: the most popular blogs and bloggers, the most popular topics, and the different styles that bloggers use.)

Just go to Google and create an account, or log in if you already have one and get the free reader. Go to your favorite sites and look for an orange button indicating a feed. Then you put the RSS feeds of your favorite sites into the Google Reader. Sometimes this process is automated so you will be asked how you want the feed delivered and in this instance you would select "Google Reader." This will save an enormous amount of time for you. And I'm told successful bloggers peruse a *huge* number of sites daily. (I could give you some numbers, but it can get kind of scary how much the top bloggers read and how hard they work.)

2. **Shortcut—Press This!: Post from wherever you are on the web** With this bookmark you can add to your toolbar, which provides a fast and smart popup to write posts to your WordPress blog as you're surfing the web

The Press bookmarklet is found at the right bottom of the Write Posts panel. Drag and drop it onto your Favorites, Bookmarks, or Links list or toolbar. To activate, simply click on the "Press It" bookmarklet link. A window will open with the uniform resource identifier (URI) of the current site displayed, and the site's title as your post title. Here's what it looks like:

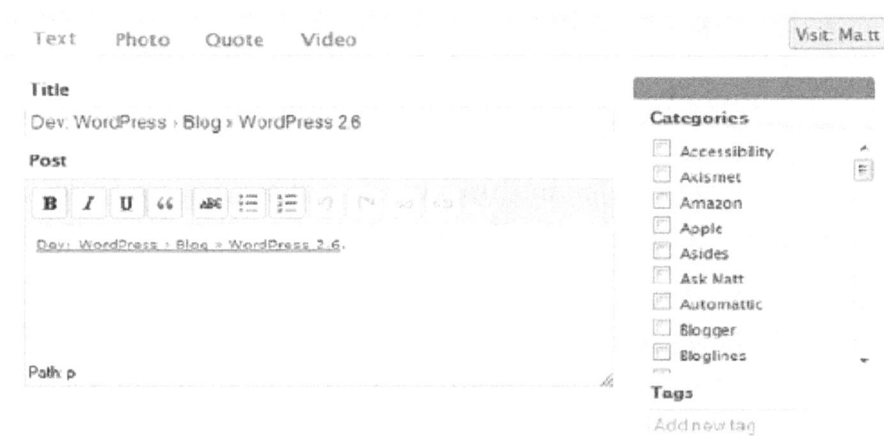

For example, if you click "Press This" from a YouTube page, it'll magically extract the video embed code, and if you do it from a Flickr page, it'll make it easy for you to put the image in your post. Not to mention, you can use it with regular text posts where you just copy and paste the portions you want to comment on, and write your own thoughts. and voila! You're done.

Well, not exactly done, if you really want to take your blog to another level, make it more useful and have it stand out; consider using the Zemanta plugin, which I consider almost an editorial assistant.

3. **Zemanta** enables you to blog smarter with instant smart links, pictures, tags, and more. The ability to automatically add a relevant graphic to the top or bottom of your blog adds interest for your users. Also, as Zemanta puts it:

> **Save Time ...** with relevant content from all over the web delivered instantly as you blog.
>
> **Build Traffic ...** with immediate tagged links created between your posts and others sharing related conversations.

These features bring increased value to your blog. Plus using these fast and easy techniques will build your confidence and get you moving in the right direction ... toward a higher level of blogging. Blogging better translates into increasing user engagement, number of users and, ultimately, revenue, if you've monetized your blog with relevant value-add products or services.

Frequency of Publishing: Develop a System

The media landscape on the Net has changed. In order to maximize the opportunity of amplifying your website's signal in this shifting media landscape, you must think strategically about how publishing can help you achieve your goals and objectives. With some planning, transforming into the "publishing is marketing" model is achievable for any individual.

Individuals and marketers have always published content, but it's the landscape that has changed, not the concept of publishing. It is the way that the content that we publish is delivered and consumed, the way that it moves around the social web, and is globally syndicated that is different. This landscape has also opened other forms of content for organizations and individuals to produce; specifically, you can now add audio, podcasts, and video content to the already rich mix of blog posts, articles, white papers, research, and surveys; you can host webinars and Google+ hangouts. These are mediums that once had a large barrier to entry and were commonly associated with heavy production budgets. Not anymore.

The challenge is how to produce a continuous flow of blog posts, white papers, research briefs, surveys, webinars, audio, and video. These are some of the core published products that any individual can take advantage of in the new media landscape. Each one serves a key role to the overall marketing mix, and each can be seamlessly promoted using the tools of the social web.

That leads to the question, how do you create a publishing machine that stays, not only on schedule, but also stays aligned with your marketing, sales, or self-promotion objectives?

One of the first and foremost considerations is your talent. Can you write well? Then write a blog post. Can you talk intelligently about your product, service, or industry? Then hit the record button and publish a regular podcast. (For a step-by-step tutorial on how to start podcasting, using all free tools to begin, go to Learn How to Podcast 101). You can actually make a video just using your iPhone. Putting it up on your website will boost traffic by as much as 10 percent. The barriers to entry are just too low not to be taking advantage of these mediums. All that said, content is still key.

You might find it challenging, at first, to organize your content creation processes, but that will become a matter of habit. To compete in a crowded blogosphere and get noticed, and more important, respected for your viewpoint, you must publish on a frequent basis. That's what the most popular pros do. And with a little focus and determination, you can become one of them

Where to Look for Fresh Content

Identify the thought leaders in your field. One way to do this is to go to Alltop. Creator and tech guru, Guy Kawasaki, describes Alltop as "an information filter to help you find your nuggets of gold." He also characterizes Alltop as "an online magazine rack of topics ranging from A to Z, which displays the headline and five most recent stories from each source."

In running AdvancingWomen.com, I most frequently went to the careers section. But, whichever section is most akin to your interests and the subject of your website, you will find ample material to get your creative juices flowing. You can also identify the authors you consider "thought leaders" in your field.

For more in-depth information, you can visit the websites, look for the orange RSS button, and get the feeds for a jumpstart on blog topics to write for the day. You can also quote from or comment on the posts extensively, or with a short sentence, including a link to the post.

Curating Content

> Content curation is "the process of analysing and sorting Web content and presenting it in a meaningful and organized way around a specific theme."
>
> — Macmillan Dictionary

This type of selection and repurposing process has come to be recognized as very valuable on the web. For one thing, according to Eric Schmidt, CEO of Google, "Every two days now we create as much information as we did from the dawn of civilization up until 2003." That's a vast amount of content to sift through and none of us can do it all. That's why we appreciate the discerning eye of "curators," analogous to museum curators, who can sort through the chaff and pick out the kernels of information that add value to a specific theme.

As web guru Guy Kawasaki put it in his Kindle book, *What The Plus! Google+ for the Rest of Us,*

Be a curator.

> I salute anyone who can regularly generate content that's informative analytical, helpful, amusing, or amazing. This is called "blogging." I did it for a few years, but I couldn't sustain blogging because I have a wife, four kids, one dog, two chickens, two turtles, three guinea pigs, and two lizards.
>
> By necessity I became a curator, which means that I find good stuff and point people to it. Curating is a valuable skill because there is an abundance of good content but many people don't have the time to find it. The best curators find things before anyone else does.

Guy Kawasaki is one of the best at discovering useful content and that's one reason people follow him. Another is his generosity in sharing how to do various things on the web and the thoroughness and clarity that he brings to his subject matter. He is an ideal person to emulate if you wish to build a following, because you will be solving problems for your users.

Twitter Feed

One way to automate curated content for your blog is to use Twitter Feed. Be sure you have segmented your audience by their interests. For example, I used to cover several different topics on Advancing Women so I had a number of different Twitter accounts, each covering just one topic: @gretchenglas covered the latest developments in tech news; @advancingwomen covered career strategies, tools, and resources.

As you begin, you may have just one topic you cover, and, in that case, one Twitter account that relates to it. Once you have identified authors you consider "thought leaders" on that topic in your field, you can go to their websites, look for the orange RSS button and get their feeds. You can then set up a Twitter Feed account, which will automatically post these RSS feeds as tweets.

I suggest you go to Alltop, with its A-to-Z listed topics and check out the top news sources or bloggers in your field. Decide who you most admire, consider the most interesting, informative, lively, or a thought leader in your field. You will have to go to the website and look. Then set up a spreadsheet with the name of the author, the title of the news source, website or blog, and the URL of the website.

Then, because the next steps can easily be completed by a virtual assistant, VA, I would contact TaskRabbit or another VA, as this is what I've always done. Provide them with your spreadsheet and login credentials to both your Twitter Account and your website, and have that person set up a Twitter Feed account in your name, go to the websites you've listed, look for the RSS Feed, and insert it into your Twitter Feed account. When it is complete, ask your TaskRabbit VA to integrate it with the Tweets flowing into your website.

Occasionally add manual tweets, which will also flow into the Tweet section of your website, thereby guaranteeing fresh content for your site every day, which is a "hands-off," automated technique that builds both website traffic and your authority on a particular subject.

As individual tweets are added to pages, you are also building your page volume. Because the widgets you've placed on a sidebar appear on every page, and you should have revenue producing ad and affiliate links in your sidebar, your continuous tweeting should also be increasing your revenue. This has a compounding effect over time.

List.ly

Another resource that can be a big help is the List.ly plugin. As pointed out on the site:

> "30% of all web content are lists or contain list content. Listly is the infrastructure that makes this content social."
>
> —Shyam Subramanyan

> "Lists & collaboration are in our DNA. Listly connects these two core human traits in an app that's as social as a campfire."
>
> —Nick Kellet

- You can share lists or embed them in your WordPress page. Just click on the "Embed This" icon. You will see four choices, depending on whether you want to embed the full list, a short version, or header only. On the screens that appear you can either grab the WordPress short code or the JavaScript code. Copy and paste it in and you have a new page on your blog, which you can edit as suits you. You can even get a List.ly plugin to add, edit, and embed lists, using a short code on your pages. It doesn't get much easier than that.

Here's a link to an example:

- 20 Terrific Twitter Tools

CHAPTER 6

MARKETING / SOCIAL MEDIA / SALES

HOW DO I LET MY PROSPECTS/STAKEHOLDERS KNOW I'M HERE?

Reinforce and Broadcast Your Brand

Self promotion is part of the game of business. The difference between business success and business failure often has more to do with effective self-promotion than with technical competence. If you want recognition, you must start promoting yourself. No one is going to know any of your achievements, if you don't tell them. As someone once said, "Modesty does not create opportunity." **Learn to tell your own story.** Learn to weave your successes into a pithy story, which becomes as much a part of your repertoire as a handshake. Sit down and write your story, the times you've succeeded, what you've achieved, and times you've made a difference. That's the story you need to commit to memory and weave into all your public speaking—even your casual conversations with colleagues and even in your briefest "elevator pitch," something you can convey between the seventh and second floor on an elevator when sharing it with a mover and shaker. **Determine to become a master of the visibility game.**

Attend networking events with the movers and shakers in your niche. Tell your compelling, engaging story to them, and let them help you tell it to a broader circle.

One of the reasons small business people often fail to market is that it can appear to be such a large and daunting task, something intimidating enough to seem to require expert skills from big marketing firms. It doesn't have to be either daunting or intimidating, particularly on the web. Marketing is not just the rollout of new General Motors or Starbucks or Target campaigns. Marketing is also a lot of small actions, which, taken together, can create awareness for your business or your brand.

Marketing can be a simple press release sent out on the web, but reaching hundreds of websites and news sources. Marketing can be getting your product mentioned or, one by one, developing links to your website. Marketing is anything that gets out the word about you and your product and gets people to try it. Think of it as Starbucks thinks of a $5 coupon for coffee—something small and manageable that will encourage a customer to walk through the door, or through your "virtual front door" on the web. And, as enough customers do, you will build momentum and increase the scale of your marketing. The important thing is to start and to make it a regular practice, part of your every day, week, or month routine.

How to Drive Traffic

Every day when you write a new blog post or page, you should post a link to Twitter, Facebook, Google Plus, and possibly Pinterest. Use IFTTT, IF This, Then That, to automate the process.

Market Your Blog

Launching your blog is essential, but making it visible to the world is equally critical in order to drive traffic and ultimately make your blog profitable. Once you have your

WordPress blog setup and populated with content, it's time to market it!

In Guy Kawasaki's Kindle book, What the Plus! Google+ for the Rest of Us, in a section titled "Perceptions, People, Pictures, or Passions, "Kawasaki says," The key to social media is to use the right tool for the job." He notes, however, the tools are not mutually exclusive. In other words, it all depends on how you want to use them.

According to Kawasaki,

> **Twitter = Perceptions.** Twitter is great for getting or sending immediate perceptions such as witnessing news and events ...
>
> **Facebook = People.** Facebook is the way to learn what's going on in the lives of people you already know (family, relatives, and colleagues) ... **Pinterest = Pictures.** Pinterest is an online bulletin board where people post pictures of what they consider beautiful, cool, and neat ...
>
> **Google+ = Passions.** Google+ enables you to pursue your passions with people you don't know."

I think **Twitter** is also a good channel for identifying "thought leaders in their fields," and leveraging their views and thoughts by commenting on their posts or adding their RSS feeds to your Twitter Feed, and from there to your blog Tweets.

Facebook has a huge audience, but as far as your marketing is concerned, your own Facebook page still addresses your family and friends, so it might be good to launch a product or service to people you already know but not to keep spreading the word and expanding your market. You can, however, create a Facebook page for your business and use it to market to a targeted demographic. Ben and Jerry's, Starbucks, and Coca Cola are examples, although there are plenty of small businesses like yours and mine.

Pinterest is growing exponentially, has gained almost 50 million users and is now used by most of the world's top 100 brands. If visuals could work well with your product, you might want to explore it further. I haven't developed a Pinterest strategy yet, but I understand a good place to start is Pinterest Power: Market Your Business, Sell Your Product, and Build Your Brand on the World's Hottest Social Network [Kindle Edition]

LinkedIn

LinkedIn is the social network for professionals, to let the business world find you, know who you are, and your professional accomplishments. You can also use it to get introduced to other professionals in companies you are interested in. LinkedIn dramatically increases your visibility on the Net, which is what you want for both you, as a professional, and your website.

LinkedIn enables you to write your own profile, which is accurate and which you have control over, so that is the first place potential clients and colleagues go when looking for information about you. (It is not a website showing you wearing a party hat with your nieces and nephews climbing on your shoulder as your dog is kissing your ear and you are struggling not to trip over your cat.)

Sales Are Where the Rubber Meets the Road

Timothy Ferriss, author of the hugely popular The 4-Hour Workweek, recommends what is perhaps his favorite piece of marketing advice: "If you only have time to read one article on marketing, make it 1,000 True Fans by Kevin Kelly, founding editor of *Wired Magazine*."

Kelly discusses how artists, creators, and entrepreneurs can escape from the intense competitive pressure of the "long tail," which, according to Wikipedia, describes "the retailing strategy of selling a large number of unique items with relatively small quantities sold of each—usually in addition to selling fewer popular items in large quantities. The long tail was popularized by Chris Anderson in an October 2004*Wired* magazine article, in which he mentioned Amazon.com, Apple, and Yahoo! as examples of businesses applying this strategy. Anderson elaborated on the concept in his book *The Long Tail: Why the Future of Business Is Selling Less of More*. Kelly reasons,

> One solution is to find 1,000 True Fans. While some artists have discovered this path without calling it that, I think it is worth trying to formalize. The gist of 1,000 True Fans can be stated simply:
>
> A creator, such as an artist, musician, photographer, crafts-person, performer, animator, designer, video maker, or author—in other words, anyone producing works of art— needs to acquire only 1,000 True Fans to make a living.

A True Fan is defined as someone who will purchase anything and everything you produce. They will drive 200 miles to see you sing. They will buy the super deluxe re-issued hi-res box set of your stuff even though they have the low-res version. They have a Google Alert set for your name. They bookmark the eBay page where your out-of-print editions show up. They come to your openings. They have you sign their copies. They buy the t-shirt, and the mug, and the hat. They can't wait till you issue your next work. They are true fans.

Creative Commons License

Kelly goes on to quantify this by reasoning that a True fan will spend a day's wages on your products or $100 a year. So if you accumulate 1,000 fans, you will earn $100,000 a year. By leveraging your unique content and affinity with your True Fans, you will also be nurturing lesser fans, and they might, in fact, move one day into the True Fan category. If they do, you could have a giant hit. But even if they don't, you are able to make a good living with 1,000 True Fans. Link to a sales page to convert your users to customers. If you are selling an affiliate product, you will be provided with links to landing pages. If you are selling your own product or service, you will need to create your own "landing" or "sales page." To make the task easier, be sure you have all the right elements, such as benefits and a "Call to Action" on the page.

If you think you need more firepower and want professional software to do a lot of the heavy lifting for you and generate landing pages with many additional helpful elements, you should look at LeadPages This membership site will generate Launch and Conversion pages that are professionally designed to boost your opt-in rate, collect your subscribers' data, easily coordinate with Facebook, and provide you with actionable stats and analytics. (Tracking your analytics is the key to being able to zero in on what's working and what's not, then doing more of what's working.) LeadPages costs $27 a month, with some less expensive plans by the year. But they do have a 30-day free trial, so you can test if it will be a good investment for your site. Many professionals do consider it a good investment .Other landing page solutions are Unbounce, Optimize Press 2.0, and Instabuilder. If these are beyond your budget in the beginning, you can Google search for pages, such as 25 Best HTML Landing Page Templates for free templates.

Advertising

One of the most cost-effective ways to generate traffic is through a Google AdWords campaign. This is a pay-per-click, PPC, service: you only pay if people click on your ad and go to your website. It doesn't guarantee a sale, but it certainly does drive a boatload of traffic to your site. This is all about bidding on certain keywords from Google, which Google then uses to drive traffic to your site: As Google explains it:

- **Google search and search partner sites**: When you build your ad groups, you select keywords relevant to the terms people use when they search, so your ads reach customers precisely when they're looking for what you offer.
- **Google Display Network**: If you've chosen to show ads on Display Network sites, AdWords uses your keywords to place your ads next to content that matches your ads. Google's technology scans the content and web address of a web page and automatically displays ads with keywords that closely match the subject or web address of the page. For example, on a webpage that includes brownie recipes, AdWords might show ads about chocolate brownies or delicious dessert recipes.

You can use Google AdWords itself to get click-and-cost estimates of various keywords and also get traffic estimates for a list of keywords. You can use automatic bidding on keywords by setting the most you will pay for a keyword. You can also set your daily budget so the whole process is automated. But, the trick to using Google AdWords, is to make a profit doing it. Because you will be bidding on keywords, the keywords most in demand will be the most expensive. You should try to look for keywords that will bring the same type of traffic, but are less frequently used so they will be less expensive. Throughout a campaign, I constantly monitor each keyword's performance and eliminate the keywords that don't perform well.

Your budget should be determined in part by the price of the item and the profit you make on selling it. Not every item is a good candidate for advertising on Google AdWords because of the expense. For example, I wouldn't want to advertise a $2.99 Kindle book, from which the author nets $2.00. My employment recruiting site, Careers Advancing Women.com, could easily support, let's say, a $500-permonth budget because it would only have to sell three 30-day postings at $170 to cover that. The increased results would generally be many times more than that.

One of my clients rents vacation homes in Santa Fe for a minimum of about $2,800 per home. She can afford to invest a great deal more in advertising on Google AdWords. In fact, by managing her adwords with the concentration of an Indian firewalker, I managed to get her ads to show up at the top of the first page of Google, which was her dream goal.

SEO Chat provides a tutorial on buying Google AdWords.

Using this system, you can soon figure out your conversion rate. For example, if one out of every hundred people who clicks through "converts," that is, becomes a customer and buys whatever you are selling, then you know how much advertising you need to reach a certain goal. If you have a high-end product or service, Google AdWords, along with your own content marketing, is a good bet for producing more revenue for you.

CHAPTER 7

SCALING UP AND OUTSOURCING THE DELEGATION IMPERATIVE

This path, selling services is a lot more time intensive than selling a product. There are two ways to slip out of those time chains. The first is to think like a lawyer or doctor does when he sets up his office practice. Break everything down into its smallest component parts and delegate or outsource each to the most basic level that can get the task done with minimal effort. Save yourself for the "Crown Jewel" moment—such as the moment you actually get to see the doctor. This is how Apple funnels its work process through its retail stores. You go online and input your Apple ID and let's say make an appointment with the "Genius Bar." You click on the type of device you're having the problem with: Mac? iPhone? The screen then displays the available time slots and you pick one. You can then input what kind of problem you're having. At this point, Apple, or its computers, already knows who you are, has all your personal data, and knows which device you're having problems with so you can be routed to some-one trained in this device.

Once you arrive at the store, you will be at the front and the Genius Bar will be at the back. Think of this as a track or a funnel, which they are going to route you through. There will be a couple of greeters at the front who smile and ask if they can help you. When you indicate you have an appointment at the Genius Bar, they say "Oh, well, then, go right over to Pamela, the girl with the red hair (or Joey, at the end of the second table) and she (he) will help you." Pamela, or whoever the person you are directed to, will be holding an iPad, where she will look up and confirm your appointment," and say, "Oh, yes, I have you right here, can you please sit at the table next to us and we'll be with you in a minute."

A minute or so later, Andy, or whoever your tech is, will come up and say "Hi, what kind of problem can I help you with today?" This is to confirm what you said your problem was when scheduling your appointment, and perhaps gather any more data before going to work, collaboratively, with you, to discover the root of the problem. Usually your tech can fix the problem in 5 to 10 minutes. If it's a much more complex problem, which is not usual, the techs will either take it in for repairs or, if your device is more than five years old and parts are no longer available, they will direct you to a reliable, nearby store that can fix the problem. They also give you directions to get there. There is no charge for the help, but if you happened to buy something while you were there, the tech you are talking to will swipe your card on his device and send you the receipt by email. The whole process has been designed to take you through it as swiftly and efficiently as possible, with no wasted motions.

Most of the time, except for a continuous process of talking to my techs on how to improve the user experience, my only interaction with the actual backend of Careers. Advancing Women site (as opposed to the blogging , content and maintain strategic alliances), is when I get a series two email notifications: one notifying me of a new job submission; a second notifying me of a payment through one of my payment gateways. The second, and possibly best, technique for reducing your workload as a professional is to develop products you can sell offering your advice: CDs, videos, audios, and white papers. You can hire others to produce these products, under your guidance and to maintain and add fresh content to your website.

For example, you can do limited and high-profit consulting and target only high profile work, such as speeches or panels at large associations to gain visibility and promote your products. You can have someone video and audio your speaking engagements and use snippets on your website for content. At the same time, you can package the longer version for sale as a product. All this can be accomplished using outsourced workers.

The Outsourcing Process

Today, there is a whole world of freelance, or outsourcing platforms. Videos of the outsourcing process can be found on YouTube. On May 5, 2015, Elance-oDesk, the world's largest freelance talent marketplace relaunched as Upwork, with millions of freelance contractors. TaskRabbit is a smaller platform with far fewer contractors. This is important because the greater number of contractors gives you a lot more selection in whom you choose to hire. Upwork has detailed time analysis features, which helps you manage the work. There is also an escrow service so your money doesn't go out until you are completely satisfied with the work.

TaskRabbit is designed a bit differently It appears, as I write this, to be located in 14 U.S. cities, but the model was begun in San Francisco as a Bay Area startup, first conceptualized (as the site explains) as a platform which "connects neighbors to get things done ... Fully vetted, entrepreneurial-minded professionals contribute their time and skills to help busy people find extra time in their days to do the things they love. Neighbors helping neighbors—it's an old school concept reimagined for today."

For example, the TaskRabbit—if there's a provider available in your neighborhood—will pick up and deliver your groceries, do your yard work, clean up your kids' birthday party, and assemble furniture. In other words, he or she does a lot of real-world, small, everyday tasks, as well as business tasks. My impression is that many of the TaskRabbits use this platform as a way of making extra pocket money after their regular work hours. I've used TaskRabbit for simple tasks, such as link checking or locating specific graphics. I've also hired a web developer from Hamburg (living in San Francisco) to correct the mapping on a subdomain of mine. TaskRabbits apparently like to work fast, so there's a quick turn around and that's a good thing. For me, the launch of Upwork, formerly Elance, was a moment that made the earth move. Upwork is a global community of freelancers who will bid for your work. But it is so much more. It is a platform for collaborative workspaces, an escrowed payment system with quality control built in; and a written archive of all the work you have done, who your provider was, and what you paid for the work provided.

I used the Upwork platform many times a day with multiple providers, each hired for specific tailored criteria for a particular job when I was building a lot of websites and developing some apps. One of the beauties of Upwork is, when you have a whole world to choose from, you can get some super specialists in whatever area you need. You first list a project description with specific and clear specifications. Then you look for a provider. Elance will suggest some, which is somewhat of a random assortment. You might want to invite some of these to offer you bids. You can then get more bids by setting certain criteria based on location, type of work, pricing, and the rating a provider has based on his or her feedback and number of jobs completed. When providers are suggested or bid on your project, you can review their portfolios and read other client's feedback on their completed work. I don't hire anyone with a rating less than 5.

You should realize you will get more bang for your buck if you choose providers from countries such as India, where a programmer might make $7 an hour. And be aware that large companies in the United States, companies like USAA, might use their own project managers, but they, as many large US companies, depend on the excellent programming skills and fast, quality results of Indian programmers.

You can then invite one, but preferably a dozen or more, up to 35 providers, to bid on a project you've created. Unless you specify that you only want bids from providers you've invited, you will receive bids from a number of providers who receive an alert that a job has just been posted in their field of expertise.

If I'm under serious time constraints, I only allow bids from those I've invited, because I don't have time to review candidates whose qualifications, portfolios, experience, and ranking might not be a close enough match for precisely what I want.

For large, ongoing jobs, such as developing a website, or website design, I prefer to deal with large companies, because then I don't have to deal with one individual getting sick, or deciding to take a vacation, or being perennially on "coffee break," which, in India, is "tea break." If one person can't work at a particular moment, the company puts someone else on it. If time gets tight, a company has the ability to throw more resources at the project. It, too, has a system, and as a bonus, you may well get a "project manager," a higher level tech who is overseeing a lot of techs who actually get the job done.

These are generally quite large and well-funded companies with a high level of professionalism and proven skills.

Even then, and with providers whose work I highly respect, I sometimes have been thrown a curveball. I had one Upwork provider, employed by a large company and overseeing a team of techs, who I worked with on large websites on almost daily basis, at that time. He told me he was taking a week off to get married. He then assured me that even though he would be out of pocket, his team member, "Abdul," would take over in his place so my projects wouldn't be delayed. I congratulated him and sent him an Amazon gift card as a wedding present. (His supervisor wrote and asked me to cancel the card and instead issue a new one to his whole team, as that was the company policy, to share and share alike. I understood they seemed to regard this as a bonus instead of a wedding present, but I did as I was asked because it seemed surly not to, and I didn't want to be argumentative about it.) However, "Abdul" worked for me for exactly one day before writing to say, so sorry, the entire team was taking off for four days for his friend's wedding. I was a bit frustrated but I understood that India is a country like Mexico, where they really get into their festivities and celebrations and one always has to keep an eye on the Indian calendar for big holidays and religious events.

When I have a critical, time-sensitive problem, such as someone has hacked my site, or injected malware, or as some say in the military, using initials only, a Whiskey–Tango–Foxtrot problem, I hire a super geek. That is, I look for someone who has a super specialty and is obsessed with and challenged to work all night, or however long it takes, to make whatever snafu has occurred go away and be sure all's right with the world again. These types of providers are invariably rare and expensive, but worth their weight in gold, because they keep you in business and are happy doing it. They would not, I expect, be happy in a super bureaucratic environment. I do not always go for the lowest bidder, but often choose the one I think can get the job done in the best way. Generally, you can get somewhat of a feel for a provider from how he responds to your project. Common sense, diplomacy, attention to detail, ability to listen to what it is you, the client want, all come into play.

I usually require a project to be done at a "set price" instead of "by the hour." This is the safest route as far as guarding your wallet and cash flow go. I have worked with large companies whose VAs, virtual assistants, were fine, but whose techs would try to tell me they took three hours on something I explained to them I could do in 15 minutes. That's the reason for set prices. However, when I've come to know and trust a provider, I will use an hourly pricing, because that removes the risk from them. When they take the risk of getting the estimate wrong, the provider invariably puts in padding or a cushion so the company doesn't get too little for the work. When I'm willing, with a known and trusted provider to pay for work by the hour, I get a better price. I have used programmers from large companies in India, and also virtual assistants from India, Switzerland, and the United States. I have used "lone-wolf" tech gurus from Paris, to Canada, to Nepal, to tame immediate and potentially disastrous problems on the Net. Ultimately, I developed teams of talented specialists: designers, technologists, and programmers who have numerous certifications attesting to their capabilities to deliver business value and improve the quality of the websites of customers with whom we dealt, with key customers in the United States, the United Kingdom, and Australia.

Although, as I've mentioned, one might have to try quite a few programmers or tech workers before finding one you want to work with on a continuous basis, working on the Upwork platform assures that you do not have to pay someone unless you are satisfied with his work. Your payment to a provider is put into escrow with Elance and it is not released until you approve the work and the release of funds. I have had several instances where the work wasn't done, wasn't done correctly, or the tech seemed to have no idea what he was doing and possibly just bid because he wanted or needed the money. In each case, I told the tech that I could not accept the quality of the work, that if anything that person had done was adequate, I would settle for that amount, and that I wanted him or her to retract the charges or I would take it to the Upwork resolution process. Without exception, though possibly some indignation, grumbling, and pleading, the provider would adjust the invoice or remove it accordingly, with no intervention from Elance. This is because, I think, providers are dependent on the Upwork platform to showcase their wares and earn a living. They don't want to look bad or even be kicked off the platform for shoddy work. And, fortunately, your objectives and instructions and the provider's work are amply documented. All your work instructions and commentary are preserved in writing in the "workroom" you share on Upwork, so it is a simple, although time consuming process, for Upwork to go in and see your instructions and the provider's response throughout the project. If the project is headed south, be sure to keep documenting that as you move along. I have had, perhaps three projects, out of many hundreds, where the work was unsatisfactory, and each time the provider withdrew the bill. Once, just lately, the response was a bit surly, but if you have documented your requests and instructions thoroughly, the provider really is not in a very good position if he or she chose not to comply with those.

Of course, the key to working remotely, without a common company culture, or same business norms a provider can draw from, is to communicate explicitly or provide examples of exactly what you want. Also, it is a collaborative process. If you are building a website for someone else for example, you have to be able to convey to your provider what your client wants, and what your own quality standards are for meeting that goal. Good communication is essential. If you are working with someone in the United States, it's relatively simple to pick up a phone and clarify any points you are working on. If you are working with a provider in India, most of your communication will be in writing and on Skype. And it is a bit more of a challenge to find a time you will both be able to talk, because you are working in completely different time zones. If you're not willing to work a little outside the box with a few more unorthodox hours, then select all your providers from time zones that work for you. There are several different sites that support you in planning meetings or tele-conferences in different time zones. One is Time and Date World Clock Meeting Planner. The following shows the best times for a meeting between me, in San Antonio, Texas, and a provider in Calcutta/Kolkata, which is 10 hours and 30 minutes ahead of my time. In essence, it shows that I have to schedule Skype calls either very early in the morning or 9pm or 10pm or later in the evening. If I wait until after 2pm my time, it has already become Saturday 12:30 am in India, so not only are you not going to talk, you're not going to get any work done either. I also keep the World Clock times of my recent providers on my iPhone, in the event, I want to contact one of them and need to check to be sure I won't be waking them out of a sound sleep: For me, this work as a web strategist came down to being a program manager

(1) managing ongoing projects, teams, and resources,

(2) dealing with the many internal business stakeholders and their management, and

(3) spending time managing relationships and deliverables from providers.

Believe me, this was a far cry from a passive income. And that is why I scaled back. There is a happy medium in here, if one can hit on it. I am a big believer in outsourcing and think it's a good way to stick to your core skill. But the trap can be that, because every kind of skill is available for hire, and you are a good project manager, you can take on too much. Just because something is possible and profitable, doesn't mean you should do it. In the end, even though you are hiring someone to execute the work, you still have to oversee it and you are ultimately responsible for the quality, completeness, and timeliness of it. It falls on you to see that the customer is satisfied. If you don't relish the thought of being a project manager, or feel that set of skills is not in your wheelhouse, there's another potential alternative. You can hire a Virtual Assistant, or VA to provide another layer of outsourcing for your website project. This is a huge time savings, and can ensure projects follow a structured and standard approach."

As mentioned, my practice has been to hire large companies through Upwork, so they generally had a project manager, even if he was referred to as a team leader. It is true, however, that it takes more than one try to find the best provider for your needs. It is also true that if a provider, a tech, for example, is really outstanding; some company from Austin or Silicon Valley is likely to snap him up and leave you out in the cold, searching for a reliable provider again.

One possible alternative which may or may not suit you. When I started on the web, I had to learn HTML coding because there was no "what you see is what you get" software. Today, there are a proliferation of software programs that, basically, put you in control and in charge of building, organizing and updating your own website, without having to call on, or pay anyone else to do the work for you. If you really want to "take the wheel" and be in charge, particularly of those many very minor updates that can come up. This can be a viable option.

One of the newest and best pieces of software out there is Elementor, https://elementor.com/ which may come bundled with a Template you purchase for your site, or be offered by your web host, as many software programs, plugins and widgets are.

As Elementor touts its software on its website: "Join our community of 8M+ professionals who build websites, collaborate, and grow together with the #1 web creation platform for WordPress." There are several offers including a free version which you can try and see if its for you. Essentially, it's a drag and drop program, which most of us can handle, but there's always a learning curve, even with the simplest new software or task. These are the features that make Elementor a preferred choice for many:

Live Drag & Drop Editor

Build and customize every part of your website intuitively with Elementor's visual builder. Zero coding required.

90+ Widgets

Achieve your design goals with a widget for every need along with full customization freedom

Pixel-Perfect Design

Create flawless websites with custom positions, padding, margins, and global settings for colors & typographies.

They do have a Template Library with over 200 templates, a marketing platform, Landing pages, and eCommerce stores. In short, if you wanted to invest the time and effort, you could do much of your work yourself, particularly your short, small chores with Elementor software and only a very minimum amount of investment and effort. On the other hand, if this seems scary or anxiety provoking or too much effort, when you prefer to focus on the big picture, building your content and marketing, then don't even think about it.

Fortunately there are online platforms that can take all those speed blocks and uncertainties out of the process and provide a generally quality and a hassle-free experience for you. You might want to consider hiring a Virtual Assistant. This is a process that works for many and allows consumers to outsource their basic office work, like word, excel, and powerpoint, (updating their website or blog, maintaining their email lists) to a global, hyper-specialized workforce. It's a streamlined approach in comparison to using a platform like Upwork. The idea is that the pain points of outsourcing are eliminated, leaving only a few friendly interactions in their place.

Pain points of a typical outsourcing situation:

- explaining your work to a foreigner
- waiting for the worker to respond
- waiting for the worker to wake up
- trying to communicate (key-word here is 'trying')
- losing time due to time zone differences/overlaps and schedules
- wasting hours on context for a job

"Virtual Assistant is a one-stop resource for all your Virtual Assistant needs. (They present themselves as) the web's first and largest site dedicated to reviewing Virtual Assistant companies, and helping you find the right virtual assistant to meet your unique needs. https://www.virtualassistantassistant.com/virtual-assistant-reviews-ratings For large projects, all of the above pain-points might still be worth it to accommodate the cost benefits of outsourcing. Also, if you like your tech provider and his or her work on your website, you may want to use them indefinitely and, eventually, you will work out a rapport and informal schedule of working together that make those pain points virtually disappear.

There is a threshold of how large of a project it would have to be to make the outsourcing concept make sense. There is somewhat of a sweet spot between a 1 day and 2 weeks for a project that really makes the outsourcing model shine. But for smaller jobs, the amount of hassle may be too much to make outsourcing a valid approach. If you want to almost eliminate yourself from the work equation entirely— except for the essential of understanding the work well enough to explain it in a short video conference or telephone call— and you are willing to pay for a VA's help, then that might be the answer for you. Someplace along this spectrum is the right solution for your outsourcing.

Perhaps that is a multisource solution: TaskRabbit, for the most simple project; Upwork, for a project that takes some time and requires multiple talented teams under one outsourced roof; and a virtual assistant, when you just want to pass it on and stay out of the way.

So, scale up and keep scaling up to make your business profitable and producing a proven revenue stream. You will see that the Pareto principle is alive and well: "80 percent of your sales come from 20 percent of your clients".

As Mark Winn states in a blog post on Linkedin, Live the 80/20 Rule, "Why work full time, when you can work only 20% of the time on the things that get you 80% of your profits? And spend the rest of the time sipping a cold beer on the beach, watching the sun go down!" (You can always make that a wine or Margarita.) When you get to the point you want to move into making a more passive income, start thinking about scaling back, not ramping up. Smaller can also be profitable when you keep your eye on the 80/20 rule.

CHAPTER 8

CONCLUSION

FINAL THOUGHTS MANAGE, KEEP SCALING UP, THEN SEEK BALANCE

Maintain Focus: Manage Your Site to Bring New Value to Your Users Every Day.

Don't get scattered or chase too many opportunities at once. Remember the advice of Esther Dyson, venture capitalist, high-tech luminary, and thought leader:

"More companies die of indigestion, than starvation. Pick one opportunity and do it well, rather than do five or six things badly ...opportunities will always be there." Focus on your core skill, service, or product. Focus on quality. If you are baking cakes, bake the best ones. If you are making a website, make it the best you can make it and one that expresses who you are, what you believe, and how you can genuinely help your users A true entrepreneur develops an ability to focus like an Indian fire walker.

It is not so much calm in the face of crisis, as the ability to focus on eventual success and therefore on the next step and the one after that and the best way to get through the immediate firestorm. An entrepreneur plays the odds, like a poker player. She knows that if she has a good concept, does a few things, but the right things, well, she will likely win in the end. With that inner confidence, the entre-epreneur holds the possibility of failure at bay, views crises as minor bumps in the road, and puts in all her chips, betting on the final outcome.

Scale Up

In order to keep scaling up, you will have to keep adding valuable content to your site every day. You will have to keep enhancing your own visibility and authority, which you can do by offering to speak at events; posting photos or press clippings; creating videos hosting webinars or Google+ hangouts; developing podcasts; producing Kindle ebooks on your subject of expertise; and commenting or guest posting on other authority blogs. With the email list you've developed, you can now monetize other related products or create your own information products or ebooks to market. If you need help, turn to Upwork, TaskRabbit, or Fiverr to outsource. You develop the concept and oversee it. Let your provider execute the actual detailed work. Finding an ideal provider for different tasks you require will take some trial and error. But, eventually, you should develop a team of different specialists you can rely on for various types of tasks.

Up to a certain point, you should be able to delegate work, so that your business is still mostly passive revenue for you. If you get beyond this point, you can always make the decision to scale back to a level of work and income stream with which you are comfortable.

Develop a Systems Approach and How Cloud, Collaboration, Automation and Software Can Help Big companies develop a system for doing things and small companies can do the same.

In fact, small companies have an even greater need to develop a systems approach, because they don't have the resources to be constantly making fresh decisions to handle recurring events, not to mention recurring crises, which canresult from lack of structure. Everything that can be made into a routine should be, from the moment the voicemail system answers the phone, to the moment the customer or client completes the purchase and you, and possibly your outsourced staff, complete the project. Every conversation, message, process, and interaction should be recorded, a procedure developed and followed, and a log kept on the process. IFTTT can automate that process for you.

Try to develop a policy, procedure, or guideline for every conceivable situation that will occur in your business. Invest the effort and energy to do this, and your time will be freed up for more important tasks. It will be easier to hand off to a "virtual assistant," when the time comes that you need one. It will be easier to outsource tasks, because you already have a description of the process ready. The regular day-to-day running of the business will be reduced to a routine. The definition of a "routine" is that it makes people with no management training capable of doing what it took only you, with experience and great effort, to figure out how to accomplish in the beginning. It is a routine that puts down in systematic, step-by-step form, what a capable woman learned in surmounting yesterday's crisis.

A well-managed business is one where workflow is organized, procedures are followed, and there is a process at work. Crises or even urgent situations are kept at a minimum, and when they do occur, you are free to deal with them. To help you achieve that goal Inc. has picked out some "best of breed" backoffice software, and front office software to keep things running smoothly and humming along. You can explore the links below at your leisure. But I will start you off with this piece of basic advice from Inc:

Project Management, Collaboration and Professional Services Automation (PSA) The cloud has ... ushered in online project management and collaboration.

Long gone are the days when completing a team project meant in-person meetings and scores of status updates clogging up email inboxes. Today you can collaborate on a project with coworkers, customers, suppliers or whomever by just checking into the cloud, and nobody ever has to show up in person. Small businesses can choose from scads of project management solutions that offer free and monthly subscription plans, including Basecamp, but there are now many up to date websites that compare features of various project manager systems, allowing you to select the one you think is the best fit for you. Yammer and Chatter are free social networks for business that let employees share documents, collaborate and find others who have expertise in particular areas. If you are collaborating closely with colleagues and want to keep the lines of communication open and flowing and not have to depend constantly on email, Yammer is a good way to do it. You can keep a little app open on your desktop and be instantly available for coworking.

I have to admit I am almost a Base-camp addict. Why? It keeps both my work life and my personal life projects organized and on track. Basecamp is one of those companies like Apple. If you get hooked on what it does for you, you are not likely to give it up. I readily admit I like organization and structure more than most people—and that's probably because entrepreneur's lives tend to veer off into chaos and, at the very least, result in procrastination and disorganization, if not closely monitored. So I overcompensate by putting in as much structure as possible.

Here are comments from the Basecamp website:

Who else uses Basecamp?

From freelancers, to small shops, to mid-sized companies, to enormous multinationals, Basecamp is the go-to project management tool for hundreds of thousands of groups worldwide. Check out how a shoe company used Basecamp to help open their new flagship store in Portland, Oregon." You might want to give it a try: it's free for 60 days. But don't blame me if you become a Basecamp addict as well

Basics to Remember

- Start your own business to stop trading hours for dollars and establish a passive income stream.
- Identify a profitable niche and establish your own brand.
- Create your website—bake in automation.
- It's not just a website, it's a business: know how you plan to generate revenue.
- Start to build a habit of blogging, linking back to your product or service.
- Marketing / social media—let your prospects / stakeholders know you're there.
- Know your numbers on everything: daily users, page views, most popular pages, sales, profit margins, expenses, and overhead.
- Track your numbers daily, so you can "feed the opportunities and starve the problems."
- Make improving your user engagement a continuous process and scale up.
- Once you find your most profitable 20 percent of customers, scale back down.
- Spend no more than 20 percent of your time working.

- Enjoy the other 80 percent in any way that makes you feel happy and fulfilled.

Have the Grit to Persist and You Will Succeed

Business is about problems. You will have problems to solve, day in, day out, every day you are in business. As the great manager of ITT, Harold Geneen, used to say "If you've tried 23 times and failed, you must try the 24th time. You must keep searching for a solution that is not just for the moment, but which is strategic and generic and forms a permanent solution to the problem."

You should also realize that success itself is about persistence. Not genius, or inspiration, or even abundant financing can take the place of persistence. The workplace is littered with failed geniuses or yesterday's stars who are today's old news. Persistence is the fuel that keeps the engine chugging up the hill. In the long run, it also helps to have integrity, to stick to your word with your employees and clients, who will then stick by you and your company, in both the peaks and the valleys. But to keep chugging ahead, and get past those many speed bumps, you will definitely need a large dose of persistence. Remember, you're in this for you, not for what others might think at any given moment; and you're in it for the long haul.

Whether it's a one-person shop juggling a dozen outsourced tasks, or a multi-million dollar enterprise setting new profit records, thousands of men and women today have made the decision to call their own shots, take the heat, and make the payroll, even if it's one outsourced person you've hired on Upwork or TaskRabbit. You are not alone. I hope this book has helped you. So, if you're ready, take the plunge. The water's just fine!

ABOUT THE AUTHOR

From 1996 and for the next twenty plus years, I was both web publisher and author of AdvancingWomen.com, a site designed to help level the playing field for women and likeminded men in careers, business, particularly web business, and now social media. I have provided career and business content to Fortune 500 companies, such as Citibank and Hearst, been published internationally by Cambridge University Press, by universities, military academies, medical and business societies, and financial organizations in Australia, India, and Saudi Arabia and translated into Mandarin Chinese, reaching a Chinese audience of more than two million.

I also served as financial news editor for Hearst's MoneyMinded.com/ Woman.com. I am a past member of the Board of Directors of the National Association of Women Business Owners (NAWBO-San Antonio); was active with the White House project, whose mission is to encourage women's participation in politics and to place women in the pipeline to reach the highest offices in the United States. I was also active with Win With Women, National Democratic Institute, Washington, DC. to promote women in political leadership in 65 countries and various organizations supporting the increased use and funding of technology.

I attended Wellesley College and graduated from Columbia University with a degree in writing. I come from a *very* entrepreneurial family and was, for many years, a serial entrepreneur myself, always looking for a new horizon to explore. Many years earlier, I was active in launching the wine industry in Texas which was a glorious, rewarding and very challenging undertaking. I have written a book on this: "Texas Wine Pioneers: How Texas Upset the World Wine Stage and Continues to Redefine It."

The next horizon was the dawning of the Internet, which I migrated to and set up a tent, shortly after Netscape came out with the browser in 1994. (As those of you involved with the Internet know, in Net time, that is somewhat equivalent to when the dinosaurs were crawling out of the swamps. I have many interesting stories from those wild and woolly pioneer days.) Since the commercial Internet itself was just in its infant stages, with constant, head snapping change and evolution, working on the Internet was a constant and challenging learning experience with a steep learning curve. But it's been very rewarding as well. I'm all about building community and making work faster and easier by using less money, more brain power, automation, and smart outsourcing. I hope this book will help you do the same.

Did You Like This Book?

If you like this book, please do me a favor and leave a review on Amazon.

Made in United States
North Haven, CT
20 October 2026

20740139R00075